CENTURION

VS

T-55

Yom Kippur War 1973

SIMON DUNSTAN

First published in Great Britain in 2009 by Osprey Publishing,
Midland House, West Way, Botley, Oxford, OX2 0PH, UK
443 Park Avenue South, New York, NY 10016, USA
E-mail: info@ospreypublishing.com

A CIP catalogue record for this book is available from the British Library

Print ISBN: 978 1 84603 369 8
PDF e-book ISBN: 978 1 84908 123 8

Page layout by: Ken Vail Graphic Design, Cambridge, UK
Index by Sandra Shotter
Typeset in ITC Conduit and Adobe Garamond
Map and firing ramp illustration by Peter Bull
T-55 three-way view and interior views by Ian Palmer
Centurion three-way view by Griff Wason
Originated by PDQ Digital Media Solutions, Bungay, Suffolk
Printed in China through Bookbuilders

09 10 11 12 13   10 9 8 7 6 5 4 3 2 1

FOR A CATALOGUE OF ALL BOOKS PUBLISHED BY OSPREY
MILITARY AND AVIATION PLEASE CONTACT:

Osprey Direct, c/o Random House Distribution Center,
400 Hahn Road, Westminster, MD 21157
Email: uscustomerservice@ospreypublishing.com

Osprey Direct, The Book Service Ltd, Distribution Centre,
Colchester Road, Frating Green, Essex, CO7 7DW
E-mail: customerservice@ospreypublishing.com

www.ospreypublishing.com

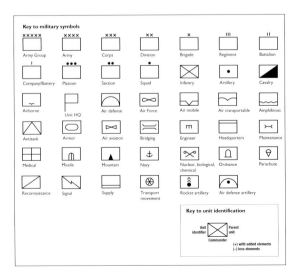

Artist's note

Readers may care to note that the original painting from
which the colour plate battlescene in this book was
prepared are available for private sale. All reproduction
copyright whatsoever is retained by the Publishers. All
enquiries should be addressed to:

H. Gerrard
11 Oaks Road
Tenterden
Kent
TN30 6RD

The Publishers regret that they can enter into no
correspondence upon this matter.

Acknowledgements:

First and foremost, I wish to express my deep appreciation
and thanks to Abraham Rabinovich for his splendid
assistance in the preparation of this book and for allowing
me to draw on his extensive researches into the Yom
Kippur War: most of these are listed in the bibliography.
I also wish to thank Michael Mass for his kind
contributions and his unrivalled expertise in all aspects
of Israeli AFVs and to Devori Borger, the curator at the
museum of the Armored Corps Memorial Site at Latrun –
Yad La'Shiryon. I am deeply indebted to Tamar Shuval for
translating obscure articles and documents from Hebrew.
My thanks also to David Fletcher at the Royal Armoured
Corps Tank Museum at Bovington for providing
information and photographs. All photographs credited to
IGPO are courtesy of the Israel Government Press Office.
Unless otherwise credited, all other photographs are from
the author's collection.

Dedication:

To Jis and Tamar

Editor's note:

Readers should note that in 1948 the British Army
changed from using Roman numerals to indicate a mark
of tanks to Arabic. Hence Mark I, Mark II and Mark III
of the Centurion but the Mark 5 onwards. Some older
units would also be re-designated post 1948.

In keeping with Israeli military conventions, US spelling
has been retained when referring to IDF units.

For ease of comparison between types of measurements
readers should refer to the following conversion chart:

1 kilometre = 0.6 mile
1 miles = 1.6km
1 metre = 3.28ft (1.09 yards)
1kg = 2.2lbs
1 tonne = 0.98 Imp tons
1 litre = 0.2 Imp gal = 0.18 US gal
1 Imp gal = 4.5 litres
1hp = 0.745kW

CONTENTS

INTRODUCTION

The tank was the dominant weapon in land warfare during World War II, supported by a myriad of other Armoured Fighting Vehicles (AFV) adapted to meet the demands of total war. Together with the essential infantryman, the tank was the basic component of every offensive from the deserts of North Africa and olive groves of Italy to the hedgerows of Normandy and jungles of the Far East. It was however on the Eastern Front that armoured battles occurred on an unprecedented scale between the forces of Nazi Germany and the Soviet Union. It was a clash of titans as thousands of tanks and AFVs fought from the gates of Moscow to the heart of Berlin. As the war progressed, the Germans produced a series of outstanding tank designs such as the Tiger and the Panther but they were overly engineered and therefore expensive to produce. As such, they were manufactured in relatively small numbers. The Soviet Union on the other hand produced a series of simple but effective designs that could be produced in vast numbers. Although its tanks destroyed a disproportionate number of Allied AFVs, Nazi Germany was defeated by the mass of war matériel arraigned against it, with the ubiquitous T-34 at the spearhead of every offensive from the East and the American M-4 Sherman from the West.

It was a lesson that became ever more significant as the post-war world devolved into mutual mistrust between the antagonistic camps of the Western Powers and the Soviet Union as codified by the North Atlantic Treaty

Organization (NATO) and the Warsaw Pact. Like the T-34, the Soviet Union was producing the T-54/55 series of tanks on a scale that the West could not possibly match. NATO therefore adopted a policy of designing tanks of superior capability to counter the Soviet advantage of numbers. Since the armoured doctrine of the Red Army remained based on the concept of an overwhelming offensive against Western Europe through the use of thousands of tanks, NATO was faced with a huge challenge. In the early 1950s, the only tank being manufactured in Western Europe was the Centurion. Originally conceived at the height of World War II,

A T-55M of the Syrian army conducts a patrol near Mount Lebanon in 1990 during the Syrian occupation of Lebanon between 1976 and 2005. This view shows the excellent ballistic shape of the turret with the 7.62mm SGMT coaxial machine gun to the left of the D-10TS 100mm main armament and the L-2G Luna infrared projector above, while forward of the commander's cupola is the gunner's TPN-1 sight. Note the crew retain the Soviet-type tank crewmen padded helmets while the commander has made himself comfortable with a large cushion at his cupola.
(Getty Images)

the design allowed for it to be repeatedly upgraded with heavier armour and more powerful main armament to maintain its qualitative lead over the T-54/55. But the fundamental question remained whether qualitative superiority could ever match quantitative superiority on the battlefields of Western Europe when the only real example was the experience of the Wehrmacht during World War II.

Fortunately, it was never put to the test in Northwest Europe but both the Centurion and the T-54/55 were sold in large numbers to client states in the continuing Cold War between East and West. During the 1960s and 1970s, one of the main arenas of superpower rivalry was the Middle East. The first major confrontation between the Centurion and the T-54/55 occurred during the Six Day War of 1967. Due to a flawed strategy and inept commanders, the Egyptian forces were totally outfought by the Israelis and no true comparison could be drawn between the tanks. In the following years, the Israelis upgraded the Centurion with a new engine and transmission for better automotive performance, as well as many other improvements, to become the Shot Cal.

It was this model that faced the Syrian army on the Golan Heights in October 1973. Equipped with a vast array of Soviet weapons, the Syrian army was trained in the classic Soviet military doctrine of 'shock action' with a total of 1,400 T-54, T-55 and T-62 tanks poised for action along a border area some 35 miles long by 15 miles deep. Beyond lay the nation of Israel. Against this massive force, the Israelis mustered just 177 Centurions divided into two armoured brigades, the 7th and 188th Barak. When battle was joined on the afternoon of 6 October 1973 this was not just another round in the cycle of Arab-Israeli wars but the ultimate test in battle of two opposing philosophies in armoured warfare – of East and West, of quantity versus quality. It was also a duel to the death of the Centurion and the T-55 that epitomized those conflicting doctrines. This is an account of one of the most extraordinary defensive battles ever conducted as 177 Israeli tanks fought for four long days against overwhelming numbers for the survival of their country.

CHRONOLOGY

1943

8 September The General Staff of the British Army issues the requirement for a new Cruiser Tank under the designation A-41, later named Centurion.

1944

August A prototype of the T-44 is completed as the successor to the famed T-34 series.

1945

April The first Centurion prototype is completed and six prototypes are despatched to Germany in the following month for combat trials, but the war ends before their arrival.

1946

Spring Production of the Centurion Mk I and Mk II begins.

1946

April A modified T-44 is fitted with a larger turret mounting a 100mm gun to become the T-54 and is accepted for service with the Red Army.

1948

Production of the Centurion Mk III with a more powerful 20-pounder gun begins.

1950–53

The Centurion sees combat with the British Army during the Korean War.

1952

Production of the definitive T-54 Model 1951 begins and is later widely distributed to Warsaw Pact countries.

The first Centurion model featured a turret with a cast front and welded rear with an independent machine gun beside the 17-pounder main armament. Six prototypes of Centurion arrived in Germany in May 1945 but too late to see action.

1954

Production of an improved model of the Centurion begins as the Mk 7. Throughout the decade the Centurion is sold to NATO-supporting countries.

1956

October The T-54 first sees combat with the Red Army during the Hungarian Uprising of October 1956. During the following month, the Centurion sees combat during the Suez Crisis.

1958

June Production of an improved model of the T-54 begins in June as the T-55.

1961

October The Centurion and T-54/55 confront each other during the Berlin Crisis.

1962

Production of the Centurion ceases after 4,423 models have been built.

1965

September The Centurion sees combat during the Indo-Pakistan War.

1967
June — The Centurion and T-54/55 face each other in battle for the first time during the Six Day War.

1968–71
The 1st Australian Task Force employs the Centurion in jungle warfare in South Vietnam.

1971
December — The Centurion sees combat during the Indo-Pakistan War as do the T-54/55/59 on both sides, although there are no encounters with the Centurion.

1973
October — The greatest battles between the Centurion and the T-54/55 occur during the Yom Kippur War.

1971–79
The T-54/59 sees extensive combat in South East Asia in Laos, South Vietnam, Cambodia and during the Sino-Vietnamese War of 1979.

1977
Production of the T-55 ceases by when some 50,000 had been manufactured.

1980–99
The T-54/55/59 sees extensive service during the 1980s and 90s in numerous conflicts in Africa, in the Nicaraguan civil war, in Afghanistan and during the protracted Iran–Iraq War of 1980–88.

1982
The Shot Cal sees combat during the invasion of Lebanon.

1987–88
The Centurion and T-54/55 see combat during the Angolan Civil War when the Olifant upgraded Centurions of the South African Defence Forces clash with MPLA T-54/55s manned by Cuban troops.

1991–1999
The T-54/55 is the principal tank employed by all sides during the Yugoslav civil war of the 1990s.

1991/2003
The T-55/59s of the Iraqi army are destroyed in large numbers during the two Gulf Wars.

2002
The Shot Cal is withdrawn from IDF service in the summer of 2002 although heavy APC variants of the vehicle continue in frontline service to this day.

2009
The T-55/59 is used during the Sri Lankan civil war and to crush the Tamil Tigers in the final battles of May 2009.

2009–present
As the Olifant Mk IB, the Centurion remains in service with the South African army to this day.

After the Yom Kippur War, the Shot Cal was progressively improved with new fire control and turret traverse systems and subsequently with Blazer reactive armour panels to disrupt infantry HEAT anti-tank weapons such as the RPG and Sagger ATGM. The Blazer armour system is shown to advantage on this Shot Cal C with its gun barrel being cleaned near Beirut during Operation *Peace for Galilee* on 16 June 1982. (IGPO)

DESIGN AND DEVELOPMENT

At the outbreak of World War II, the British Army possessed just 977 tanks across the whole of the far-flung British Empire. Worse still, only 77 of these tanks mounted any weapon larger than a machine gun. The great proportion of the army's tank inventory was made up of Tankettes or Light Tanks as these were much cheaper to produce than true tanks and more suitable for garrison duties in Britain's overseas territories or combating hill tribesmen on the North West Frontier. After a period of innovative exercises in the practice of mechanized warfare in the late 1920s, British tank design and armoured doctrine languished due to political and financial constraints. The torch of innovation passed to the Soviet Union during the 1930s, together with Nazi Germany. Ideologically wedded to the offensive doctrine in warfare, the Red Army conceived the doctrine of 'deep operations' that was conceptually similar to Blitzkrieg as devised by the Wehrmacht. Both doctrines envisaged a rapid offensive based on the integrated combination of tanks, ground attack aircraft and motorized infantry, as well as paratroopers to land in the enemy's rear areas and disrupt lines of communication. Prior to World War II, Germany and the Soviet Union produced large numbers of tanks of increasingly effective designs.

When Britain began rearmament in face of the growing Nazi threat, it lacked both the design capability and the manufacturing capacity to produce tanks in quantity. In consequence, the British Army entered World War II with a series of generally ineffective designs configured for a variety of roles on the battlefield. These included Infantry Tanks to support infantry attacks and Cruiser Tanks for mobile operations once a breakthrough had been achieved. It was a doctrine that harked back to World War I rather than the age of Blitzkrieg. Most of the army's tanks were lost during the

battle of France in May 1940 so Britain had no choice but to continue building the same types despite their known deficiencies because of the immediate threat of invasion and its widespread overseas commitments, particularly in North Africa. It was patently unrealistic to expect commercial companies to turn their hands to the design and construction of complex AFVs and produce battle-worthy models without years of experience. Conversely, the Soviet Union was producing tanks in vast quantities due to its wide industrial base. Thanks to ambitious Five Year Plans throughout the 1930s, equipment had been guaranteed as a priority for the Red Army. At the outset of Operation *Barbarossa* in July 1941, it possessed 24,000 tanks; more than the rest of the world put together. Among them was a model that was to influence many subsequent designs during World War II – the T-34.

The T-34/76 was a simple, rugged and highly mobile tank with greater firepower than most of its contemporaries. It was well suited to mass production but suffered some significant design flaws in the early versions. Nevertheless, the T-34/76 came as a rude shock to the Germans as they had nothing comparable to its excellent combination of firepower, armour protection and mobility – the three fundamental design parameters of any successful tank. In the first two months of Operation *Barbarossa*, the Red Army lost over 5,000 tanks in combat including most of the modern T-34s and KV-1s. When the frontlines stabilized at the gates of Moscow in December 1941, the Red Army possessed only 4,495 tanks of which 2,124 were stationed in the Far East. Just as the British kept building inferior tank designs after the battle of France so the Soviets were obliged to continue producing existing models to compensate for the massive losses of 1941. No modifications, however necessary or desirable, were tolerated if they interfered with production

From the Mk II onwards, the Centurion featured a cast turret with a welded roofplate. Shown during crew training with the 8th Royal Tank Regiment in Yorkshire during 1948, these are Centurion Mk IIIs with the more powerful 20-pounder gun.

The T-54/55 series has been produced in greater numbers than any other battle tank in the post-World War II era and has seen combat in more theatres of war around the world than any other tank. This T-54 was captured by the Mujahideen and used against its previous owners during the Soviet war in Afghanistan. This model has the D-10TG 100mm gun with a counterweight at the muzzle indicating that the tank is fitted with the STP-1 *Gorizont* or Horizon stabilization system for the main armament in the vertical axis. (Getty images)

quotas until the German invasion was fully contained. Accordingly, the T-34 did not see any radical improvements until after 1943 when the battle of Kursk revealed the urgent need for a more heavily armed version of the tank to counter the much feared Tiger and Panther tanks.

An improved model of the T-34 armed with a 85mm D-5 gun was accepted for production on 15 December 1943 and the first T-34/85 entered service with the Red Army in March 1944. Production of the T-34/85 was soon running at 1,200 per month at a time when there were only 304 Panthers on the whole Eastern Front. The T-34/85 was at the forefront of the climactic battles of Operation *Bagration* in the

(Artwork by Griff Wason)

CENTURION SHOT CAL SIDE-VIEW

9.83m

summer of 1944 that led to the destruction of Army Group Centre in the greatest defeat suffered by the Wehrmacht in World War II. Meanwhile, plans for a successor to the famed T-34 series were underway at the Alexsandr Morozov design bureau at Nizhni Tagil under the project codename *Obiekt 136*. The new tank was designated the T-44 and it was undoubtedly an impressive design, although early models suffered the recurring problem of many Soviet tanks of a troublesome transmission. It displayed excellent ballistic protection, with the armour of the hull and turret up to 120mm thick, with good mobility. In fact, the T-44's combat capabilities were on a par with the PzKpfw. V Panther but it weighed only two-thirds as much at just 32 tons. However, there is no record that the T-44 saw combat during the Great Patriotic War.

By 1943, the British were at last producing a worthwhile tank in the Cromwell, which featured an adequate 75mm main armament and high mobility. However its armour protection was barely adequate by contemporary standards. Coupled with the widespread use of the American M-4 Sherman, it allowed the newly formed Department of Tank Design to start with a completely clean sheet. On 8 September 1943 the General Staff issued the requirement for a new Cruiser Tank under the designation A-41. In the intractable debate in tank design as to how to combine the three basic elements of firepower, protection and mobility, the British opted for the first two, although agility across country was considered of more importance than a high road speed. The main armament of a 17-pounder gun had to be capable of defeating the Tiger and Panther at normal combat ranges. Conversely, the A-41 was required to provide sufficient armour protection against the dreaded German 88mm. This was to be achieved by incorporating a well-sloped front glacis plate similar to the T-34 and Panther. The final specification for the A-41 was considered by the Tank Board on the 23 February 1944 when they gave their full support to the project and

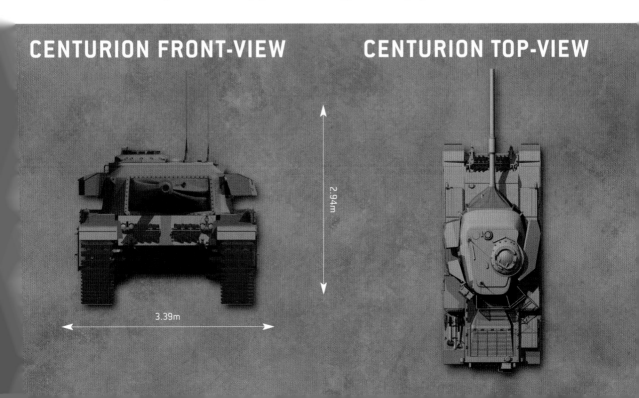

CENTURION FRONT-VIEW

CENTURION TOP-VIEW

2.94m

3.39m

ordered the production of 20 prototypes. The first A-41 prototype was delivered in April 1945 and in the following month six prototypes were rushed to Germany as part of Operation *Sentry* to test the new tank under combat conditions. They arrived just too late to see action but the trials continued and the men of the Royal Armoured Corps enthusiastically endorsed the new tank, now named Centurion, although they did note that it did not represent any real qualitative improvement over the Panther that had been introduced in 1943. Production of the Centurion began in early 1946 and the first tanks were issued to troops in Germany in December 1946.

Although a highly promising design, the T-44 still retained the same 85mm gun as the T-34/85. Attempts to install a larger weapon were not overly successful because of the cramped turret interior. Accordingly, the development of a larger turret mounting a D-10T 100mm gun began in 1945. It was fitted to a revised hull of the T-44 under the project codename of *Obiekt 137*. The first prototype was completed in late 1945 and it was accepted for service in April 1946 as the T-54. Production began in the following year but the original version suffered such serious teething troubles that production was suspended. Furthermore, the greater bulk of the 100mm ammunition meant that only 34 rounds were carried in the T-54-1 as compared to 60 in the T-34/85. Yet another turret was designed displaying a distinct similarity to the excellent ballistic shape of the IS-3 Heavy Tank with its hemispherical configuration. The new turret was accepted for service in 1949 although it still had unsatisfactory shot traps at the rear. Series production of the T-54 resumed as the T-54-2 or T-54 Model 1949 to differentiate it from the earlier model. A third and definitive turret design was introduced in 1951 with its classic bisected egg shape, the narrow end pointing forward and mounting the D-10T 100mm gun in a narrow mantlet. This version was known as the T54-3 or T-54 Model 1951.

Although the Centurion performed admirably during the Six Day War of 1967, the IAC devised an extensive upgrading programme to improve its mobility and range. The new model was designated Shot Cal and it entered service in the summer of 1970. (IGPO)

TECHNICAL SPECIFICATIONS

THE CENTURION

Both the Centurion and the T-54/55 were the synthesis of each respective country's wartime experiences of armoured warfare. For the British, the employment of different types of tanks for armoured operations was by now largely discredited. All had proved to be chronically under-gunned and inadequately armoured as the technological race for tank superiority accelerated throughout the war. While Germany was invariably at the forefront, both Britain and the Soviet Union proved superior in the field of mass production. Britain alone built more tanks than Germany during World War II, while the Soviet Union produced three times as many T-34s as all the German tanks manufactured from 1941 to 1945. A sea of steel swamped Germany as thousands of AFVs invaded the country from both the East and West. For the Red Army, the employment of separate Medium and Heavy Tanks had proved successful with hordes of T-34s at the forefront of 'deep operations' while the IS series of Heavy Tanks provided direct fire support in the assault while their powerful 122mm guns proved devastating against German armour: hence their nickname of 'Animal Killers' for destroying Panthers and Tigers. For the British Army there was little consolation as, to the end, the majority of its tanks remained deficient in firepower to counter the latest generation of German tanks. Fortunately, the latter were few and far between in the final days of the war. Lurking anti-tank guns, self-propelled guns and hand-held infantry weapons such as the *Panzerfaust* caused the majority of tank casualties. Nevertheless, the perception remained that British tank crews were at a distinct disadvantage in any tank-versus-tank duel. It was a sentiment that gave rise to the

determination never to allow British tank crews to enter battle with inferior firepower or armour protection to a potential enemy.

To this end, the Centurion had been undergoing many improvements following its entry into service with the British Army. Like the T-54, the Centurion was fitted with a new turret design of improved ballistic protection and better layout for the crew in the Mk II version. More importantly, the revised turret was able to mount the new 20-pounder (83.4mm) gun that was superior in performance to the D-10T 100mm main armament of the T-54, particularly when firing the new APDS or Armour Piercing Discarding Sabot ammunition. Introduced in 1948 as the Centurion Mk III, this was the definitive early model of the Centurion and its technical description is as follows. The Centurion Mk III was of conventional layout with the driving compartment at the front, the driver on the right and the main armament

T-55 SIDE-VIEW

9m

T-55 FRONT-VIEW

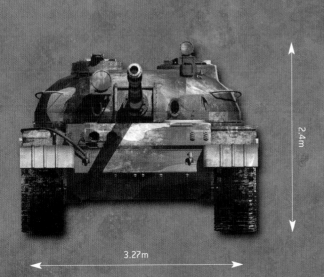

2.4m

3.27m

T-55 TOP-VIEW

The Mk III with its 20-pounder main armament and coaxial Besa machine gun was the definitive model of the Centurion with 2,833 being produced between 1948 and 1955. At the peak of production, 11 Centurions were manufactured each week but at the same time the T-54 was being made at the rate of 44 a week.

ammunition stowage to his left. The fighting compartment was in the centre of the hull with the rest of the four-man crew – the commander, gunner and loader/radio operator – in a fully rotating power-operated turret containing the main armament and coaxial machine gun, together with the radio equipment. To the rear behind a dividing bulkhead were the engine and transmission compartments, as well as the cooling fans. With a fully laden combat weight of 50 tons (112,000 pounds or 50,803kg), some 44 per cent of the Centurion consisted of armour, 11 per cent armament and ammunition, 5 per cent for the engine, 30 per cent for the transmission, suspension and tracks while the remaining 10 per cent was made up of the crew, stowage and other items such as fuel.

The driver sat on the right-hand side of the front hull with his two viewing periscopes in the access hatches in the hull roof above his head when driving closed down. The driving controls comprised the clutch, brake and accelerator pedal arranged conventionally left to right with the long gear-change lever mounted centrally. To each side of his seat were the steering levers. As one was pulled backwards so the relative speed of the tracks altered and thus the direction of travel of the tank. As all the controls were linked to the engine and transmission by mechanical rods, the Centurion demanded much physical exertion and constant concentration to ensure a smooth passage to the rest of the crew across broken country. With thorough training, a good driver was able to achieve a sustained cross-country speed of some 15mph with minimal crew discomfort, ensuring that they arrived at a point of contact in a fit state to fight. The driver's duties included undertaking first-line maintenance of the tank such as cleaning air filters and tightening tracks.

The crew commander was situated at rear of the turret on the right-hand side with a vision cupola above his position providing all-round observation from under armour. He was also provided with X10 binocular periscope for precise target acquisition. Forward of him was the gunner's position with his gun controls, periscope sight and range gear to his front and right. The Centurion was the first tank to be equipped with a full stabilization system for the main armament and coaxial machine gun in both azimuth and elevation. Previous systems such as fitted to the M-4 Sherman were only stabilized in elevation. For the first time this allowed the tank to fire on the move with both the gunner and commander having full control in this mode. It is particularly effective when firing the coaxial machine gun in a prophylactic manner against entrenched infantry when advancing at speed. When engaging enemy armour, it was quite feasible to track a tank accurately while on the move but it was often

A Shot Meteor and a Shot Cal undergo comparative trials in the Negev Desert.

17

A Shot Cal manoeuvres over the broken ground of the Golan Plateau. With its rugged Horstmann suspension, the Centurion was better suited to the difficult terrain of the Golan whereas the M-48/60 Magach series, with its torsion bar suspension but superior speed, was more suited to the sands of the Sinai Peninsula. Furthermore, the heavy frontal armour of the Centurion was deemed an asset in the defensive battle envisaged from the prepared positions along the Purple Line as well as for any offensive into Syria that would, perforce, be on a narrow axis. (IGPO)

better to then stop and make final adjustments to the lay of the gun to maximize the chances of a first round hit: a process known as 'firing from the short halt'. Once the target was struck, the Centurion then moved off at speed while the commander acquired another target.

The Ordnance Quick Firing 20-pounder Tk Mk I and the coaxial 7.92 Besa machine gun were both served by the loader/operator positioned to the left of the main armament. By contemporary standards and the T-54 in particular, the internal volume of the Centurion was more than adequate to allow the crew to undertake their tasks efficiently. All the rounds of ammunition were stowed below the level of the turret ring to increase survivability. Statistical analysis of tank casualties of World War II showed that 60 per cent of tanks that stowed ammunition in the turret suffered catastrophic fires when penetrated and that 60 per cent of all tanks penetrated were struck in the turret. In addition, British designers opted for an all-electrical turret traverse system since this was safer than those powered by hydraulics, although it is more bulky and somewhat slower. Unlike Soviet tanks where the commander operated the radios, the loader fulfilled this function in the Centurion, hence his title of loader/operator. This allowed the commander to concentrate on his specific duty of directing the tank and any others under his command. The loader/operator also had the vital function of supervising the 'boiling vessel'. This device, peculiar to British tanks from the Centurion onwards, provided a constant supply of hot water for the endless cups of tea demanded by tank crews and for the warming of ration packs in the field. It also provided a modicum of heat in the turret during winter exercises on the bitterly cold north German plains.

The engine compartment was divided from the turret by a fireproof bulkhead. The Meteor Mk 4B V-12 petrol engine developed 650bhp giving a top speed of 21mph and, thanks to its high torque, commendable agility across country. Power from the main engine was transmitted via the clutch to the Merritt-Brown Z51R gearbox. The transmission comprised a combined steering and braking mechanism that drove the rear-mounted sprockets. The complete power plant was highly reliable, if used regularly, although it did suffer from high fuel consumption. This gave rise to the major criticism of the Centurion with its inadequate range of approximately 50 miles before refuelling was necessary. The vehicle featured a Horstmann-type suspension with three units, each of four road wheels, per side. Being externally mounted to the hull, these did not encroach on the internal space of tank as torsion bar systems did and were easier to replace following mine damage. The suspension units and the hull sides were protected from infantry hand-held anti-tank weapons by three detachable skirting plates that gave the Centurion its distinctive profile, as did the stowage bins around the turret.

Operational experience in West Germany and during the Korean War had shown the need to increase the radius of action of the Centurion since in heavy going across country the range on one filling of fuel was as little as 30 miles. As an interim measure improvised fuel drums were mounted on the rear hull plate followed by a less successful mono-wheeled fuel trailer holding 200 gallons. In late 1952, a comprehensive redesign of the Centurion hull was undertaken to increase the amount of fuel stowed under armour. Production of the Centurion Mk 7 began at a new Ministry of Supply factory run by Leyland Motors in 1954. In the following year, the decision was taken by NATO to standardize on the .30-inch or 7.62mm calibre for small-arms ammunition. This led to the replacement of the 7.92mm Besa coaxial machine gun of the Centurion with the

19

M1919A4 Browning. With this modification, the tank became the Centurion Mk 5. A Mk 4 had been planned, mounting a 95mm close-support howitzer, but it was never produced. Meanwhile, a new turret was under development with a revised mantlet featuring resiliently mounted gun trunnions, improved gun control equipment as well as a new commander's contra-rotating cupola that allowed faster target acquisition and incorporated a double leaf hatch to give overhead 'umbrella' protection to the commander while allowing him direct vision of the battlefield: a device subsequently adopted by the Israelis as the 'Tal cupola'. When this new turret was eventually mounted on the revised hull with its extended range, the model became the Centurion Mk 8 in 1956.

From 1959 onwards, the Centurion underwent an up-armouring and up-gunning programme whereby an extra 2 inches of armour were added to the glacis plate to give greater immunity against the 100mm main armament of the T-55. This involved the substitution of the 83.4mm 20-pounder with the L7 105mm gun that, because of its outstanding performance, became de facto the standard main armament within NATO. When both these modifications were applied retrospectively to previously built models, the Centurion Mk 5 became the Mk 6 while the Mk 7 and the Mk 8 became the Mk 9 and Mk 10 respectively. New-build vehicles had these features incorporated during production. The final two modification programmes for the Centurion in the British Army were the fitting of IR night-fighting equipment and a coaxial-mounted .50-calibre ranging gun together with a thermal sleeve for the 105mm barrel. The Centurion hull also became the basis for a series of special purpose variants to undertake a variety of roles on the battlefield including an armoured recovery vehicle, various bridge layers, an assault vehicle for combat engineers mounting a 165mm demolition gun and a version for use on amphibious beach landings. Together they showed the great versatility of the basic Centurion design but, interestingly, the Israeli Armored Corps did not procure such variants in any quantity as gun tanks were deemed to be paramount and the defence budget did not extend to such luxuries on the battlefield.

SHOT CAL – THE SCOURGE OF THE T-55

Even before the Six Day War, the IDF Ordnance Corps was addressing the deficiencies of the Centurion. In particular, its limited operational range and low speed were deemed to be the main disadvantages, although its firepower and armour protection were greatly admired and appreciated. Many parents of sons entering the IAC demanded that they be assigned to Centurion units, as it was believed that they would have a greater chance of survival in battle. The ageing Meteor engines had to be repeatedly rebuilt, while ease of maintenance and engine replacement times in the field were long and arduous in the Centurion and overburdened the repair facilities. The auxiliary assemblies, particularly the cooling system, posed frequent maintenance problems. In the desert, radiators became clogged with sand and oil while pulleys and drive belts failed with increasing regularity. The original air filters proved to be only partially effective in the Negev Desert unless they were flushed with fuel and filled with fresh oil daily or in extreme conditions after every four hours of operation.

To overcome these problems, the Ordnance Corps devised an upgrading programme to improve its performance and reliability following its experience with the M-50 and M-51 Sherman conversions. In the words of the official publication by the Ordnance Corps on the project:

> What prompted the IDF, after having used the British Centurion Mk 5 for a number of years to perform such an extensive operation and to completely reshape the old 'battle horse'? The answer can be summed in one sentence: the necessity to bring the Centurion Mk 5 which was built in the early '50s to the first line of the tanks of the '70s in regard to performance, reliability, maintainability [*sic*] and ease of operation.

The primary requirement was to replace the gasoline-powered Meteor engine with a more fuel-efficient diesel power plant. The choice of engines suitable in terms of power, speed and operational range was limited to six, but none of these would fit in the existing engine compartment. During the course of development, three different engines were tested. Although all three alternatives were successfully installed and trialled, the Teledyne Continental AVDS-1790-2A air-cooled diesel was selected primarily due to standardization with the M48A2C Pattons that were being similarly modified in a separate upgrading programme. The adoption of this diesel engine had a number of further advantages including its ready availability on the international market, its lower fuel consumption by a factor of 1.7 and reduced fire risks in combat. At the same time, the Merritt-Brown Z51R gearbox was replaced by the Alison CD-850-6 automatic transmission that greatly eased the task of driving, particularly across country, and simplified driver training.

As the selected power pack was too large for the existing engine compartment, the rear hull had to be enlarged. Even so the engine was installed at an inclination of 3.5 degrees, front side up, giving the characteristic hump shape of the back decks. Because of the increased fuel capacity requirements, intricately shaped fuel cells were developed to utilize all available space. Among the numerous other modifications were a more efficient oil-cooled braking system; fire extinguishers in the engine compartment of greater capacity, with a 10-second delay on actuation to allow the cooling fans to stop so that they did not disperse the extinguishing agent before it took effect; and increased ammunition stowage of 72 rounds, with more of them readily accessible to the loader. In all, it took three years to develop the upgraded Centurion at the former British Army barracks of Sarafand, later the IDF Ordnance Corps depot at Tel HaShomer, near Tel Aviv. The tank was given the name Shot Cal or 'Whip' in Hebrew and earlier versions were designated Shot Meteor until such time as they were upgraded as well. The first Shot Cal entered service with the IAC in May 1970 and it soon saw combat during border incidents with Lebanon and Syria and during the War of Attrition along the banks of the Suez Canal. Within just one month of entering service, the Shot Cal fought its first major action when the 188th 'Barak' Brigade conducted a raid into Syrian territory in June 1970 during a four-hour battle with a Syrian tank brigade in which 36 T-55s were destroyed. But the Shot Cal was to fight its most desperate battles during the opening hours of the Yom Kippur War of October 1973 – once again in the hands of the Barak Brigade.

THE T-55

After its unhappy debut, and once the problems with the transmission were resolved, the T-54 proved to be a worthy successor to the T-34 series that had been largely instrumental in achieving victory on the Eastern Front and the eventual triumph over the remaining forces of the Third Reich in the battle of Berlin. Starting in 1949, the T54/55 series was built in greater numbers than any other post-war battle tank with over 50,000 rolling off the production lines. The T-54 entered series production in 1953 and the T-54A was introduced in 1955. The T-54A had a revised D-10TG 100mm main armament that featured stabilization in the vertical axis with the STP-1 *Gorizont* or Horizon system. The D-10TG also had a fume extractor near the muzzle fume, based on the bore evacuator design of captured US M-26 and M-46 Medium Tanks from the Korean War. This model was also manufactured in Czechoslovakia, Poland and in China as the T-59. Two years later, the T-54B appeared with full stabilization for the main armament that was now designated D-10T2S. The system was known as the STP-2 *Tsiklon* or Cyclone. In April 1959, infrared (IR) night vision and fighting equipment was introduced for the commander, gunner and driver. Intriguingly, the Centurion featured full stabilization from its earliest models in 1947 whereas the T-54/55 series achieved it only in 1957. Conversely, Soviet tanks were fitted with IR night-fighting equipment several years before their NATO counterparts. Total production of the T-54 series was approximately 24,750 in the Soviet Union with 5,465 in Warsaw Pact countries and a further 9,000 in China under the designation T-59.

Hundreds of T-54/55 tanks have been used in the countless wars that have ravaged the continent of Africa to this day, from Angola to Sudan and from Ethiopia to Eritrea. This T-55A(M) was sold by Ukraine to the Democratic Republic of the Congo in 2006 and is being prepared for action on 26 October 2008 against the renegade forces of Laurent Nkunda that had captured the village of Rugari, some 40 kilometres north of the provincial capital of Goma. (Getty Images)

In October 1955, a comprehensive improvement programme for the T-54 was initiated under the designation *Obiekt 155*. The principal innovation was the introduction of protection against Nuclear, Biological and Chemical (NBC) contamination on the nuclear battlefield that was now deemed to be inevitable by Soviet planners in any future conflict. The new design was accepted for service in May 1958 and production ran from June 1958 to July 1962 in the Soviet Union and subsequently in Czechoslovakia and Poland. The T-55 was of conventional layout with a four-man crew. Like the Centurion, the wartime practice of a five-man crew with a hull machine gunner, such as the T-34 or Cromwell tanks, was dispensed with in the interests of extra ammunition stowage, given the increased size of the main armament ammunition. However, the crew positions were reversed to those in the Centurion and, indeed, most Western tanks. The driver was situated in the left-hand side of the hull front while the commander and gunner were positioned to the left of the D-10T gun and the loader to its right.

The most striking aspect of the T-55 was its compact dimensions with a height to the turret top of just 2.39m although the loader's roof-mounted heavy machine gun did somewhat compromise the low profile: in comparison, the M-48 stood 3.13m tall and the Centurion 2.94m. However, the superb shaped turret did markedly reduce the internal volume of the tank and make it extremely cramped for the crew. This inevitably affected their performance when fighting closed down over extended periods of time. It also significantly reduced overall ammunition stowage with just 43 rounds as against 65 for the Centurion. Nevertheless, such a compact tank was difficult to hit and the armour configuration made it more likely for shells to ricochet off the turret or glacis plate without penetrating, while the limited amount of ammunition carried was compensated for by the sheer numbers of Soviet tanks committed to any offensive. For these reasons, Soviet tank crews were chosen on

account of their short stature with anyone over 1.68m in height being uncomfortably too tall for the task.

The hull was constructed of welded rolled armour plate with vertical sides and a well-sloped glacis plate with interlocking joints for increased ballistic integrity. The 'driver/mechanic' in Soviet terminology sat in the left-hand side of the hull front with an access hatch in the hull roof and an escape hatch in the floor behind his position. Like the Centurion, the T-55 required considerable effort to drive with its basic mechanical controls and five-speed gearbox that required repeated gear changes when travelling over broken terrain. Such simplicity was typical of Soviet tank designs as it reduced procurement costs but at the price of reliability, often due to clutch failures. To the driver's right were the vehicle batteries, a fuel tank for the diesel engine and ammunition stowage for main armament rounds. As Soviet tanks had to operate over a vast temperature range including in the depths of a Siberian winter, the T-55 was equipped with a compressed air starter for the engine with an electrical system as a back up.

The V-55V 580bhp liquid-cooled V-12 diesel engine was mounted transversely at the rear and power was transmitted to the drive sprocket at the rear with the idler at the front. The T-55 featured a torsion bar suspension system with five double rubber-tyred road wheels per side with a distinctive gap between the first and second road wheel stations. With a power to weight ratio of 16bhp per ton (as against 13 for the Centurion), the T-55 had a speed of 50km/h on roads and up to 30km/h across country. It had a range of 500km on its integral tanks with a further 200km when fitted with the external fuel drums at the rear below which the tank usually carried a wooden unditching beam. Following World War II experience and the many river crossings that the advance into Germany entailed, the T-55 could be readily fitted with a snorkel for deep wading. Two types were developed, a thin one for operational use and a wider one for training exercises that allowed the crew to escape in an emergency. The OPVT fording equipment allowed the crossing of rivers up to five metres in depth and 700 metres wide with navigation by an onboard gyrocompass. Such a device was very much in keeping with the Soviet doctrine of the offensive whereas no Western tank designs had this feature except on an experimental basis.

The commander and gunner were positioned to the left of the D-10T2S 100mm gun with its breech mechanism filling a large proportion of the turret interior. The ready-rack of ammunition rounds on the rear wall compounded space limitations and there were further rounds on the hull walls as well as under the gun and floor. The gun featured full stabilization of the main armament and electro-hydraulic traverse of the turret. By Western standards, the gun control equipment and sighting devices were rudimentary, with the commander acquiring a target through his TPK-1 designator sight. He then traversed the turret in line with the target and gave the gunner an estimation of the range by the graticule pattern of his stadiametric sight. He then gave the loader the ammunition selection depending on the type of target. The gunner

The T-55 was the first Main Battle Tank designed to operate on the nuclear battlefield and fight under conditions of NBC contamination. It was also able to operate in the severest of climatic conditions as shown here as a formation of T-55s undergoes winter manoeuvres during the 1970s; a scene so reminiscent of its illustrious predecessor the T-34 fighting on the Eastern Front during the Great Patriotic War. (RAC Tank Museum)

SHOT CAL CENTURION

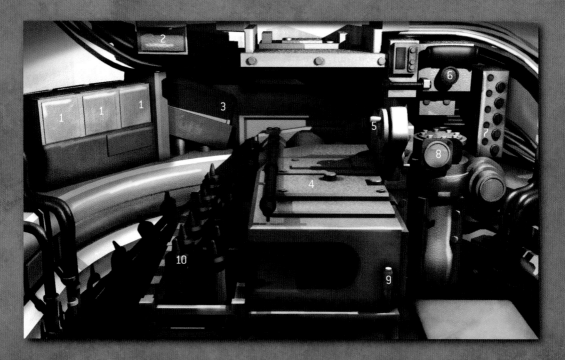

1. Spare boxes 7.62mm ammunition
2. Loader/operator's periscope
3. Coaxial machine gun and ammunition box
4. Breech of L7 105mm main armament
5. Elevating handwheel
6. Gunner's sight
7. Gun control equipment
8. Turret traverse indicator
9. Breech opening lever
10. 105mm ready ammunition rounds

Crew: Four
Combat weight: 50,728kg
Power/Weight ratio: 12.81hp/tonne
Ground Pressure: 0.9kg/sqcm
Length overall: 9.829m
Length hull: 7.556m
Width: 3.39m
Height: 2.94m
Ground Clearance: 0.457m
Max road speed: 34.6km/h
Road range: 102km
Engine: Meteor Mk 4B 12-cylinder petrol of 650hp
Transmission: Merritt-Brown Z51R manual with five forward and two reverse gears

Suspension: Horstmann
Armament: 1 × 83.4mm 20-pounder & coaxial 7.92mm MG
Ammunition: 65 rounds 20-pounder & 3,600 MG
Smoke laying: 2 X 6 smoke grenade dischargers
Gun elevation: +20 degrees −10 degrees

Armour
Turret front: 152mm
Hull glacis: 76mm
Hull nose: 76mm
Hull sides: 51mm
Hull floor: 17mm

T-55

1. Commander's sight
2. Turret traverse handle
3. Gunner's sight
4. Gun control equipment
5. Breech of D-10T2S 100mm main armament
6. Gun recuperators
7. Coaxial machine gun
8. NBC filtration system
9. Breech opening lever
10. Turret traverse indicator

Crew: Four
Combat weight: 36,000kg
Power/Weight ratio: 16.11hp/tonne
Ground Pressure: 0.81kg/sqcm
Length overall: 9m
Length hull: 6.45m
Width: 3.27m
Height: 2.4m
Ground Clearance: 0.425m
Max road speed: 50km/h
Road range: 500km
Engine: V-55 V-12 diesel of 580hp
Transmission: Manual with five forward and one reverse gears

Suspension: Torsion bar
Armament: 1 × 100mm 20-pounder & coaxial 7.62mm MG
Ammunition: 65 rounds 20-pounder & 3,600 MG
Smoke laying: Diesel fuel injected into exhaust system
Gun elevation: +17 degrees – 4 degrees

Armour
Turret front: 203mm
Hull glacis: 97mm
Hull nose: 99mm
Hull sides: 79mm
Hull floor: 20mm

then made the final fine lay on the target with his TSh 2-22 sight with a magnification of X3.5 or X7. He fired when ordered to do so by the commander. The main armament was capable of firing the following types of ammunition including AP (Armour Piercing), APC-T (Armour Piercing Capped Tracer), HEAT (High Explosive Anti-Tank), HE-Frag (High Explosive Fragmentation) and subsequently APDS (Armour Piercing Discarding Sabot). The usual ammunition load was two-thirds High Explosive (HE) and derivatives and one third armour piercing.

Meanwhile, the loader was trying to manipulate another round, weighing in the region of 50 pounds, into the opened breech as the tank bucked across country. His position was so cramped that most loaders had to ram home the projectile with their left fist, which made the task even more difficult. The loader was also responsible for the coaxial machine gun in the turret; originally the 7.62mm SGMT and subsequently the 7.62mm PKT machine gun. Like the T-54, the early production models of the T-55 featured an SGMT fixed rigidly in the centre of the glacis plate that was fired by the driver: a legacy of the wartime bow gunner of the T-34. It proved to have limited tactical value and the driver/mechanic was usually too busy to bother with it. Accordingly, it was discontinued from the T-55 onwards and the space saved taken up with a further six rounds of 100mm ammunition. The T-55 was also the first model to have a fully rotating turret floor that made the loader's tasks somewhat easier in the confines of the turret.

Undoubtedly, one of the most significant tactical disadvantages of the compact configuration of the T-55 was the lack of depression of the main armament at just −4 degrees rather than the typical −10 degrees of Western designs. This meant that it was extremely difficult for a T-55 to obtain a satisfactory hull-down firing position with just the turret roof and gun barrel visible to the enemy but again, as Soviet doctrine stressed the offensive, this shortcoming was deemed to be acceptable. A further serious limitation of such poor ergonomics was that the loader was hard pressed to load more than four rounds a minute when a proficient NATO tank crew was expected to fire the same number within the first 15 seconds of an engagement. In one demonstration, the crew of a Centurion Mk 5 armed with a 20-pounder gun fired 15 rounds in 43 seconds at 15 different targets and hit every single one at ranges between 800 and 1,000 yards. These fundamental design differences were to have a significant effect during the fighting on the Golan Heights in October 1973.

As with most successful designs, a range of special-purpose variants was built on the T-54/55 chassis. In particular, a number of armoured recovery vehicles that could also assist in deep-fording river crossing operations. Other variants included the bridge-laying vehicles also modelled on the T-54/55 chassis. As part of its offensive armoured doctrine, the Soviet army also employed several mine-clearing devices for the T-54/55 series by fitting gun tanks with rollers or ploughs to disable anti-tank mines. Typical systems included the PT-55 mine roller and the KMT-4 mine plough or a combination of them both with KMT-5. The KMT-5 or Kolesniy Minniy Tral was the standard mine-clearing system in the Soviet army from the late 1960s. It was this type together with the MTU bridge layers that spearheaded the Syrian offensive on the Golan Heights in October 1973.

COLD WAR COMBATANTS

By 1953, both the Centurion and the T-54 were in full-scale production. However, the volume of production was hardly in the same league. In Britain, the Centurion was manufactured at ROF Barnbow in Leeds and at Vickers-Armstrongs at Elswick, near Newcastle upon Tyne, at the rate of 11 a week. In the Soviet Union, the 1951–55 Five Year Plan authorized the production of no less than 11,700 T-54s for the Red Army or 44 a week from the Nizhni Tagil UVZ Tank Plant No.183 in the Urals and the Kharkov No. 75 Tank Plant in the Ukraine. It was to be a keynote production throughout the Cold War. The ability and determination of the Soviet Union to produce scores of thousands of tanks based on this offensive doctrine could only be countered by the Western Powers through tanks of technological superiority: it was to be an unproven equation of quality versus quantity in a contest of the highest stakes between the NATO powers and the Warsaw Pact controlled by the iron fist of the Soviet Union. In microcosm, the Cold War was reduced to a duel between individual tank crews exemplified by the Centurion and the T-54/55. Both tanks were to see combat in every corner of the world except in the region for which they were originally designed to fight – Northwest Europe. Many of these conflicts across the globe were but a projection of the prolonged Cold War between East and West and their respective ideologies. The most dangerous crucible of superpower rivalry was to be in the Middle East, where the Centurion and the T-54 were to fight their fiercest battles.

The Centurion first saw action during the Korean War of 1950 to 1953 in terrain and temperatures that were to test the tank's agility to the full. As part of the United Nations Forces deployed to respond to the communist invasion of the Republic of Korea, an armoured regiment of 45 Centurions manned by the 8th King's Royal Irish

The first occasion when the Centurion and the T-55 met in hostile confrontation was during the Berlin crisis of October 1961, following the construction of the Berlin Wall. These tanks are a mixture of T-54 and T-54A models at the Friedrichstrasse checkpoint at the height of the confrontation on 25 October. (Getty Images)

Hussars supported the British Army contingent. It was at the battle of the Imjin River in April 1951 that the Centurions of the 8th Hussars won lasting fame when their tanks covered the withdrawal of the 29th Infantry Brigade in heroic fashion in the face of the overwhelming Chinese spring offensive. Once the fighting became static, the Centurions proved their worth on many occasions when they acted as direct fire

On the other side of the city divide were the Centurion Mk 5 tanks of C Squadron, 4th Royal Tank Regiment, acting as the Independent Tank Squadron of the Berlin Brigade.

support to the infantry units facing human wave assaults from the Chinese army. The reputation it gained in Korea for its combination of firepower, armour protection and agility in such difficult conditions led to the procurement of the Centurion by several NATO nations through the US Mutual Defense Assistance Program, including Denmark and Holland with further sales to Australia, Canada, Egypt, India, Iraq, Israel, Jordan, Kuwait, New Zealand, South Africa, Sweden and Switzerland.

While the Korean War was still raging, the Centurion saw action in the Suez Canal Zone in 1952 to quell Egyptian insurgents and armed militia fighting for independence from the British. In a similar vein, but on a far greater scale, the T-54 first saw operational service during the Hungarian Uprising of 1956. The revolt began on 23 October and lasted until 10 November, coinciding almost exactly with the Suez Crisis and the Second Arab-Israeli War. On 24 October, Soviet tanks surrounded the Parliament building in Budapest but fighting soon erupted between armed Hungarian militia and the hated ÁVH secret police. On 3 November, the Soviet army launched Operation *Vikhr* (Whirlwind) and invaded Hungary with some 17 Soviet divisions, occupying Budapest in force the following day. During the fighting, Hungarian freedom fighters captured a T-54 and it was inspected by the military attaché from the British Embassy. He was able to glean such vital information as the thickness and inclination of the armour configuration and many aspects of its interior that had previously eluded Western military intelligence.

The T-54/55 was first used operationally by the Soviet army during Operation *Vikhr* to suppress the Hungarian Uprising of 1956. On 24 October, these T-54 and T-54A tanks surrounded the Parliament building in Budapest. Here, Tank 230 is a T-54A with a D-10TG main armament with fume extractor while Tank 232 is a basic model T-54 with a D-10T 100mm gun. (Getty Images)

Jordanian tank crews of the 40th Armoured Brigade prepare their Centurion Mk 7s for action prior to the battle of Ramtha on 22 September 1970 against the Syrian 67th and 88th Armoured Brigades of the Syrian 5th Infantry Division that invaded Jordan In support of the Palestine Liberation Organization. In the first encounter between Centurions and T-54/55s of Arab armies, the Syrians lost 62 tanks out of a force of some 300 T-54/55s as against 19 Centurions knocked out in action.

Intriguingly, the US Army deployed an 'A' Team of Green Beret Special Forces to the Austrian border ready to capture a T-54 that had been identified just 28 miles inside Hungarian territory but the operation was never authorized.

Both the Centurion and the T-54/55 were primarily designed for high intensity warfare in Northwest Europe but the closest they ever came to combat in that operational theatre was during the Berlin Crisis of 1961. Following World War II, some 15 million people fled Soviet-occupied Eastern Europe to the West. To stem such an exodus, the Inner German Border was created in 1952 as a real manifestation of the Iron Curtain, with barbed wire fences and armed patrols. Thereafter, the main route for East Germans to escape to the West was through Berlin. By 1961, almost three and a half million East Germans or 20 per cent of the entire population had fled to the West. On Sunday 13 August, East German troops began the construction of a barrier to divide the city that became known as the Berlin Wall. Soviet tanks were massed on the border to discourage interference by the Western Powers or riots on the streets. Tension rose in the coming months culminating in a confrontation between fully-armed M-48 and T-54 tanks at the Soviet checkpoint on Friedrichstrasse on the afternoon of 27 October. Both sides had orders to open fire if fired upon. Centurion tanks of the Berlin Brigade were also placed on high alert and deployed on the streets of the city. Overnight negotiations between the White House and the Kremlin produced a face-saving formula. On the next morning, one Soviet tank followed by one American tank each reversed some five metres until the streets were clear and the troops returned to barracks.

The next major conflict fought by the Centurion was with the Indian army during the Indo-Pakistan War of September 1965. But the first major confrontation between Centurions and T-54/55s occurred during the Six Day War of June 1967. The T-54/55 was employed once more by the Soviets to crush another Warsaw Pact country when tanks of the 6th Guards and 35th Motor Rifle Divisions entered Czechoslovakia on the night of 20/21 August 1968 to suppress the 'Prague Spring' under the guise of 'fraternal assistance'. Centurions went to war again with the 1st Australian Task Force in South Vietnam between February 1968 and January 1971. In the same year, Centurions fought in the Indo-Pakistan War of 1971, as did the T-54/55. India was equipped with the T-54A and the T-55 while the Pakistani army fielded the T-54A and the T-59, the Chinese licence-produced version of the Soviet T-54A. However, there were no tank-versus-tank battles between Centurions and T-54/59s. During the Jordanian Civil War of September 1970, the Centurions of the 40th Armoured Brigade countered a Syrian invasion by the 5th Infantry Division reinforced by two armoured brigades and a brigade of the Palestine Liberation Army. On 20 September 1970 at the battle of Ramtha, the Syrians lost 62 tanks out of a force of some 300 T-54/55s, mainly to the 20-pounder guns of the Centurion Mk 7s and some to Hawker Hunter fighter-bombers of the Royal Jordanian Air Force. But the greatest confrontation between Centurions and T-54/55s was to occur in October 1973 during the Yom Kippur War on the Golan Heights only a short distance from Ramtha. Here this great test between the classic tanks of the Cold War era would be determined ultimately by the superior abilities of individual crews.

The Centurion first saw combat during the Korean War of 1950–1953 in a completely different theatre of operations for which it was designed. It proved highly effective despite the appalling cold weather and the mountainous terrain. A Centurion Mk 3 of A Squadron, the 8th King's Royal Irish Hussars, transports Australian infantry across the Imjin River in April 1951, when the Centurions of the 8th Hussars won lasting fame in the decisive battle that thwarted the Chinese Spring Offensive.

TANK CREW TRAINING

In the 1970s, the induction of civilians into the IDF was the responsibility of the General Staff Manpower Branch. It was implemented by an Induction Administration whose task was to turn callow teenagers into soldiers to fill the ranks of all services of the IDF. There were four periods of induction each year, in February, May, August and November, once a person, male or female, reached the age of 18. The conscript's first experience of the IDF was at a reception centre to the east of Tel Aviv where he or she spent four days being interviewed by placement officers from each of the constituent corps of the IDF. The recruit was allowed to specify three choices for assignment in order of preference but the final decision lay with the IDF in all cases. Recruits were then assigned to a specific arm or corps where they underwent further medical and psychological examinations to determine their suitability for placement depending on a designated profile. Thus, the top percentile of 97 and above was assigned to the IDF elite formations such as fighter pilot units within the Israeli Air Force. The Infantry did not admit anyone under a score of 80 and those wishing to join the paratroopers needed much higher, while the Israeli Armored Corps (IAC) required a minimum of 72. Those with technical qualifications were assigned to specific units, such as air traffic control, as the IDF deemed fit. In the IAC, the recruit then underwent four months of basic training in the Armored School before being sent to a regular tank unit to undertake his three years of service, or two for a female. It was during basic training that each recruit showed particular aptitude or not,

The Chinese produced a version of the T-54A in large numbers and it entered service with the People's Liberation Army in 1959, giving rise to its designation of T-59. It remained in production until the early 1980s by when some 8,000 were built with many sold for export, particularly to Pakistan and latterly to Africa.

whether it be driver, loader or gunner. In general, those with the greater hand/eye coordination were chosen as gunners since tank gunnery was paramount within the IAC. Once the arcane skills of tank gunnery had been mastered, a crewman became eligible to qualify as a tank commander. In this way, there were always two gunners in a tank crew in order to maximize the benefits of multiple crew skills. It was in the field of tank gunnery that the IDF excelled and crews regularly trained to engage targets out beyond 2,000 metres range. Furthermore, IDF tank crews possibly fired more rounds of live ammunition than any other army at the time thanks to their rigorous gunnery training, which was implemented in the years immediately preceding the Six Day War. It was this that gave them the qualitative edge over their opponents.

While the IDF was a citizen army and serving a civic duty, the Syrian army was based on mass conscription of all males from the age of 18 for three or four years, depending on their given task within the armed forces. Many high school graduates and those from families with influence often obtained deferment or exemption from military service, thus diluting the skills base within the armed forces at a time of 60 per cent adult literacy for males and just 20 per cent for females. Once conscripted, all Syrian recruits underwent a severe regime of basic training of 14 weeks before they were allocated to units by drafts rather than aptitude. Those assigned to tank units were often allocated to crew tasks based on their physical stature and strength, given the ergonomic drawbacks of Soviet tank designs; thus someone short but strong would be made a loader. By choice, most Syrian tank crew trainees wished to be trained as drivers since this gave them a particular skill and qualification in civilian life after leaving the army. While the majority of its modern weapons were of Soviet manufacture, the process of translating Russian technical and tactical manuals into Arabic was never fully implemented by the Syrians and mostly futile for an army of largely illiterate conscripts. Training was done by rote and on the most simplistic level: for instance, tanks crews were required to stop to engage the enemy and then fire only two rounds before proceeding with the mission. Live firing of tank ammunition was the exception rather than the rule and tactics were largely based on 'follow the leader'. Tactical flexibility was lacking at all levels. Nevertheless, what might have been lacking in finesse was more than made up for by mass, illustrating that Syria had imported Soviet doctrine as well as Soviet tanks.

Czech patriots bombard a T-54A with petrol bombs on the streets of Prague during Operation *Danube*, the Soviet invasion of Czechoslovakia, in August 1968. The white stripes on the glacis plate and turret were a mutual recognition device for the Warsaw Pact forces used in Operation *Danube*. The rear external fuel drums were vulnerable to petrol bombs and burned fiercely, as here, but did not necessarily disable the tank. Note the hole in the glacis plate for the barrel of the 7.62mm machine gun that was operated by the driver. (Getty Images)

STRATEGIC SITUATION

THE 100 HOURS WAR

Prior to the Yom Kippur War of 1973 Israel and her Middle East neighbours had engaged in a number of conflicts. In many cases armour had been the key to the decisive battles and in the decades prior to 1973 there had been a protracted arms race throughout the region fuelled by the Cold War. Immediately before Second Arab-Israeli War of 1956, the Israeli Armored Corps (IAC) was painfully aware of the limitations of its principal tank, the M-4 Sherman. This was exacerbated by the massive arms deal of 1954 between Egypt and the Soviet Union that saw numerous AFVs being introduced into the inventory of the Egyptian army. Among them was the powerful IS-3M that could not be penetrated by the IAC's most numerous tank, the standard M4A1 armed with a 76.2mm gun that was known as the M-1 Sherman in Israeli service. As soon as the Israel Defense Forces (IDF) learnt of the Soviet arms deal, they approached the French for a means to up-gun the M-1 in a similar manner as the Sherman Firefly of World War II fame. By 1955, a prototype vehicle was produced by the Atelier de Bourges arsenal. It mounted the French CN 75-50 75mm gun, as fitted to the AMX-13, in a heavily modified Sherman turret on an M4A4 chassis. A modification programme began during early 1956 in Israel: it was to be the birth of a fledgling Israeli tank industry. The first new M-50 Sherman was delivered to Company Bet of the 82nd Tank Battalion of 7th Armored Brigade for user trials and it saw combat during Operation *Kadesh* in the Sinai. The M-50 also equipped two tank companies of the 27th Reserve Armored Brigade during the assault on the Gaza Strip on 1 November 1956.

The Israeli Armored Corps had never purchased special-purpose variants of the Centurion in sufficient numbers due to cost, preferring to spend funds on gun tanks instead. In particular, Armoured Recovery Vehicles were in short supply so recovery tasks often fell to gun tanks such as these two Shot Cals: a procedure that could overload the transmission of the towing tank. (IOP)

The 100 Hours War that resulted in the conquest of the complete Sinai Peninsula was undertaken in collusion with Britain and France. Both countries wished to regain control of the Suez Canal after it had been nationalized by President Gamal Abdel Nasser of Egypt. The Israeli invasion of the Sinai was used as a pretext for an Anglo-French amphibious landing at Port Said at the northern end of the canal with the intention of occupying the whole Suez Canal Zone. As part of the Order of Battle, the British Army included a complete armoured regiment – the 6th Royal Tank Regiment

Both the Centurion and the T-54/55 saw action in the same month of November 1956 when the Soviet army crushed the Hungarian Revolution and an Anglo-French force made an amphibious landing at Port Said to occupy the Suez Canal Zone. Here, Centurion Mk 5s of B Squadron, 6th Royal Tank Regiment, patrol the streets of Port Said after the ceasefire. The Mk 5 was essentially the same as the Mk 3 but had a .30-calibre Browning coaxial machine gun in place of the Besa.

– equipped with Centurion Mk 5s. The initial assault landing of 6 November 1956 was supported by C Squadron, 6RTR, whose Centurions were fitted with deep wading equipment and came ashore with the first wave of Royal Marine Commandos. The Centurions of 6RTR were intended to thwart any Egyptian army counterattack with its recently supplied Soviet T-34/85s and IS-3Ms or even the Centurion tanks supplied by the British in 1954. In the event, only a few SU-100 self-propelled guns were encountered and no armoured engagements ensued although the Centurions of 6RTR gave invaluable fire support to the Commandos throughout the day until a ceasefire was imposed by the United Nations at the instigation of the United States. Under intense political pressure, the Anglo-French forces departed Port Said by 10 December 1956.

Similarly, Israel was forced to evacuate the Sinai Peninsula and Gaza Strip by February 1957 at the insistence of the United States and Soviet Union. Nevertheless, the 100 Hours War brought about a fundamental change in the IDF perception of armoured warfare. No longer were tanks to be used largely for infantry support. Now due to their firepower and mobility, they were to become the main striking force during offensive operations in a combined arms division-sized formation designated *ugda* that differed in configuration depending on the tactical situation or the task in hand. To this end, more capable and modern tanks than the Sherman or even the M-50 were required to fulfil the new armoured doctrine of the Israeli Armored Corps.

For political reasons, the Israeli government wished to procure M-48 Pattons from the United States so that a 'special relationship' was forged between the two nations, although America had resisted such an arrangement for many years. Even so, permission was granted for M-48A2C Pattons of the Bundeswehr to be transferred to Israel as part of German reparations for the Holocaust. A total of 250 Pattons was shipped to Israel between 1960 and 1964 including a quantity directly from the United States on a clandestine basis. Since much of the IDF's equipment including tanks and aircraft were produced in France, Israel wanted to diversify her arms suppliers as she did not fully trust any European government to be constant in the face of Arab political pressure, particularly in the provision of vital ammunition. Accordingly, Israel also approached Britain with the wish to procure Centurion tanks as a quid pro quo for her involvement in the Suez campaign. After protracted negotiations, the first shipment of Centurions arrived in Israel in late 1959.

THE WATER WAR

The Centurion was the first modern Main Battle Tank (MBT) to enter service with the IAC. At 50 tons, it was much heavier and more complex than previous tanks. From the outset, problems were encountered with the tank, particularly when operating in the training areas of the Negev Desert. The abrasive dust caused air filters to clog, leading to engines overheating and on occasions catching fire while brake failures were commonplace. Within a short period of time, the Centurion gained a woeful reputation within the IAC as temperamental and unreliable, reportedly 'more

suited to English garden lawns than the Negev Desert'. However, many of the problems were due to inefficient maintenance procedures, particularly in the field, poor driving and inadequate training. An added difficulty was that many of the Centurions bought from Britain were second-hand and in need of refurbishment and rebuilding, but at that time the Israeli Ordnance Corps did not have the facilities to undertake such major work. The majority of the Centurion models procured were the Mk 5 version armed with a 20-pounder gun. When the Egyptian and Syrian armies began to receive the T-54 in significant numbers from 1962 onwards, the IAC sought a more powerful gun for its Centurions and Pattons. The answer was found in the outstanding British L7 105mm gun. It was simplicity itself to exchange the 20-pounder of the Centurion with the 105mm gun, as well as new graticule sights and ammunition stowage racks, since the British Army had undertaken this modification in large numbers. It was somewhat more difficult with the M48A2C Patton, as this required a more complex conversion. Accordingly, priority was given to the up-gunning of the Centurion, which began in February 1962. By now the Centurion was called Shot in Israeli service, the name meaning 'Whip' in Hebrew. It first saw action along the Syrian border in November 1964 against dug-in World War II PzKpfw. IV tanks and artillery weapons dotted along the dominating Golan escarpment that fired down on the Israeli settlements in the Huleh Valley and Finger of Galilee below. These encounters showed the need for improved gunnery procedures and the new commander of the Israeli Armored Corps, Brigadier Israel Tal, rigorously imposed these. Thereafter, the Syrians tried to divert the headwaters of the Jordan River in order to deprive Israel of a large proportion of its fresh water supplies.

In what became known as the Water War, tanks were employed to destroy Syrian engineering equipment engaged in the diversion project. In time, the 105mm armed Shots proved capable of hitting targets as small as a bulldozer, at ranges out to 11km. It became the Tal credo of 'first shot, first kill, one shot, one kill' using the L7 105mm gun or 'Sharir'. Such proficiency among the tank crews of the IAC was to prove decisive in the next major Arab-Israeli war as well as the conflict of 1973.

THE SIX DAY WAR

Although the Arab attempts to divert the headwaters of the Jordan River failed, incidents continued unabated along the Syrian border. Under Soviet encouragement, Syria persuaded Egypt to sign a mutual defence pact against Israel. Tensions rose during the spring of 1967, as Arab rhetoric demanded the eradication of the Jewish state. In May, President Nasser expelled the UN peacekeeping personnel from the Sinai and heavily reinforced the Egyptian forces stationed in the peninsula. When Iraq and Jordan joined the defence pact with Egypt and Syria, belligerent and hostile neighbours surrounded Israel. In a further flagrant act of aggression, Nasser closed the Straits of Tiran to Israeli shipping. On 5 June 1967, the IDF launched a devastating pre-emptive strike against the Arab air forces and effectively eliminated them in the first 24 hours. At the same, three *ugdas* of the IDF poured into the Sinai Desert to strike the six Egyptian divisions, including the 4th Armoured Division equipped with T-54 and T-55 tanks, that were threatening Israel's border.

In the north, the 84th Armored Division or Ugda Tal under the command of Brigadier General Israel Tal attacked the heavily fortified Egyptian positions at Khan Yunis and Rafah Junction. Ugda Tal was spearheaded by the elite 7th Armored Brigade comprising 88 Centurions of the 82nd Tank Battalion together with the 66 M-48A2C Pattons of the 79th Tank Battalion. There were also Centurion battalions in the 200th Armored Brigade of Ugda Yoffe and in the 14th Armored Brigade of Ugda Sharon. The heavily armoured Centurions were invariably used to assault Egyptian positions frontally while the more mobile Pattons and Shermans manoeuvred around the flanks through the difficult sand dunes to mount attacks from unexpected quarters. One by one, the Egyptian defensive localities were attacked and overrun in a classic example of manoeuvre warfare while the great majority of Egyptian tanks were dug-in and immobile. By now the

The first combat between the Centurion and the T-54/55 occurred during the Six Day War of June 1967. Due to the inept strategy of the Egyptian high command it was hardly a fair comparison between the two tanks, with the Centurion proving vastly superior due largely to the outstanding performance of the L7 105mm gun and the standard of tank gunnery in the Israeli Armored Corps. (IOP)

A T-54 of the Syrian 17th Mechanized Brigade lies burnt out on the road to Banias after an IDF deception plan lured this elite formation of the Syrian army away from the Israeli points of attack on the Golan Heights in June 1967. This is an early model T-54 with the original D-10T 100mm gun. (IGPO)

Israeli Air Force was pounding the hapless Egyptian ground forces as the tanks of the IAC surged westwards. In the first major tank battle between Centurions and T-55s, the Soviet tanks of the 4th Armoured Division were severely mauled by 20 Centurions of the 200th Armored Brigade at the Bir Lahfan crossroads where 32 T-54s and T-55s were destroyed. Time after time, the 105mm gun of the Centurions proved devastating against the T-54/55, particularly at long ranges where the simple stadia sights of the Soviet design proved far less effective.[1]

In five days of fighting, the Egyptian army lost almost 80 per cent of its tanks during the Sinai campaign including 291 T-54s, 82 T-55s, 251 T-34/85s, 72 IS-3Ms, 29 PT-76s, 51 SU-100s, 50 assorted Shermans and some 30-odd Centurions. By comparison, Israeli losses were 122 tanks of all types. Israeli Centurions also served in small numbers on the Jordanian and Syrian fronts during the Six Day War. Intriguingly, both the Egyptians and Jordanians were equipped with Centurions, albeit the Egyptians in small numbers, but there is no evidence that there were any encounters between the Centurions of the opposing sides nor any combat between IDF Centurions with Syrian T-54/55s on the Golan Heights. It must be said that the stunning Israeli victory during the Six Day War was as much to do with the incompetence of the Arab officer corps as it was to Israeli prowess in battle. The tactical handling of armour by the Egyptian army was uniformly inept and the T-54/55 was hardly given the opportunity to prove itself on the battlefield. Hundreds of usable AFVs were captured by the IDF and many scores of T-54/55s were pressed into service with the IAC under the designation of Ti-67 or Tiran. These were progressively upgraded over the years but they never proved popular with Israeli crews because of their cramped interiors.

After the war, the commander of the 200th Armored Brigade, Colonel Yissacher 'Iska' Shadmi, had some illuminating comments to make about the campaign and his Centurion tanks:

---

1 For a fuller account of the Six Day War see Campaign 212 *The Six Day War 1967: Sinai* and
   Campaign 216 *The Six Day War 1967: Jordan and Syria* (Osprey Publishing 2009)

Although some 30 years old by the time of the Yom Kippur War, the M-50 Sherman proved highly effective against Arab armour, particularly during the battle against the Iraqi 3rd Armoured Division. This was due largely to the longstanding expertise of the Sherman crews, many of whom were in their forties and fifties and had served together for decades and so knew their vehicles intimately. Here, an M-50 recovers a companion vehicle that has broken down while a knocked-out T-55 lies abandoned in the foreground.

When I ask myself how it is possible that against the might of the Egyptian army, which my armoured columns had to face while continuously changing on the move, I was able to destroy 157 enemy tanks while our losses were almost nil – well, how did it happen? I have to give the following explanations. First of all, I agree with what has been said by the others before [regarding the superior training and tactical handling of the Israeli army]. Second, the air force. Third to my mind it was proved that the Centurion tank is by far superior to the T-55 and T-54 Russian tanks and especially in one aspect which gave our boys their self-confidence – the additional 20 tons [sic] of armour steel. And the point which in my opinion shows more than anything else how we did it were the stories about tanks that got five, six, seven hits – and there was one with 12 direct hits – and which continued to fight. But let me just tell of a few incidents. Two tanks which participated until half way through the battles, limping along on half their tracks. They were hit by mines and damaged so they shortened their tracks and were able, at a slow pace, to continue the fight. One tank was hit by a direct 120mm [mortar] shell and its turret became immobile. The officer in command decided to keep this tank at the rear and so it advanced. At the battle of Jebel Libni this tank is credited with hitting two enemy tanks.

Almost to the 1990s, the T-55 series formed over a third of the Soviet tank inventory. Accordingly, it was necessary to keep them abreast of Western designs such as the US M-1 Abrams, British Challenger or the German Leopard 2 with the fitting of a new *Volna* fire control system incorporating the KTD-2 laser rangefinder above the main armament as well as a BV-55 ballistic computer. Some of these upgraded T-55s were modified to fire the Bastion 100mm (AT-10 Stabber by Western designation) laser beam riding missile with a range of 4,000 metres and capable of defeating 600mm of steel armour protected by Explosive Reactive Armour. (RAC Tank Museum)

COMBAT

THE DEFENCE OF THE GOLAN HEIGHTS

The stunning victory in the Six Day War of June 1967 greatly extended the borders of Israel following the capture of the Sinai Peninsula and the Golan Heights together with the West Bank and the Gaza Strip. For the first time in its history Israel now enjoyed the luxury of defence in depth. The speed and scale of the Israeli victory sent shock waves through the Arab world. Israel had drawn the teeth of its bitterest enemies and its demonstration of military prowess had garnered respect around the world. Israel's position now seemed secure. However, Arab hostility remained implacable. The Khartoum conference of Arab leaders in August 1967 declared that there would

A force of Shot Cals advances across the rock-strewn ground of the Golan Heights with every commander standing high in the turret for a better view of the battlefield. This graphically illustrates why tank commanders suffered such high casualties during the Yom Kippur War from artillery fragments or strikes from Sagger ATGM and RPGs. (IGPO)

43

During the desperate early hours of the Yom Kippur War, IDF reservists rushed to their depots to prepare their equipment before climbing the Golan Heights to join battle with the advancing Syrian army. A Shot Cal follows a line of Shot Meteors showing the differences of the rear hull, turret basket and stowage position of the Xenon searchlight. (IGPO)

be 'no recognition, no negotiations, no peace' unless Israel unilaterally withdrew from the territories occupied during the Six Day War. However, these very same conquered territories now gave Israel defensible frontiers and the IDF were loath to lose them without firm guarantees of lasting security. Furthermore, Israeli public opinion was in no mood to allow the spoils of this spectacular victory to be cast aside as had happened after the Sinai Campaign of 1956.

Within weeks, however, the Egyptians resumed hostilities along the Suez Canal with heavy artillery barrages against Israeli positions. To reduce the casualty rate, the IDF were obliged to construct a static line of field fortifications on the eastern bank of the canal that fatally compromised the recently gained advantages of strategic depth for defence. It also negated Israel's superiority in manoeuvre warfare, as tanks were now

Shot Cals advance carefully towards the skyline in case of Syrian troops and tanks lying in ambush positions. This terrain and road is very similar to that which Lieutenant Zvi Greengold fought over during his heroic defensive action along the Tapline Road on the night of 6/7 October. (IGPO)

required to come to the aid of the field fortifications that became known as the Bar Lev Line. There ensued the bitter War of Attrition that continued until August 1970 but even after it ended the IDF strategy vacillated between a mobile defence of the Sinai Peninsula and a forward defence to protect the forts and occupants of the Bar Lev Line. The dilemma was never fully resolved prior to the Yom Kippur War of 1973 with dire consequences.

On the Golan Heights, the IDF faced different problems. The Israeli-occupied Golan Plateau was only 17 miles deep at its widest so a strategy of forward defence was essential as it was not feasible to trade space for time: time to allow IDF reservists to be mobilized and deployed to stem any Arab offensive. Fortunately, the volcanic terrain strewn with impassable lava flows of basalt rock favoured the defenders as only a few roads crossed the region. In addition, its numerous *tels* or extinct volcanic cones, up to 200 metres in height and overlooking the Damascus Plain where the bulk of the Syrian forces were stationed, made excellent vantage points for observation and firing positions. Only in the south was the terrain really suitable for tanks. The Israeli defences were based on the 'Purple Line' that ran from the Jordanian border in the south to the slopes of Mount Hermon in the north: the Purple Line took its name from the colour on UN maps that marked the zone of separation between the two belligerents following the Six Day War. Again, as along the Suez Canal, the ceasefire was repeatedly broken with the Syrians bombarding Israeli positions with artillery. Accordingly, the Israelis constructed a series of 12 infantry strong-points called *Mutzavim* along the Purple Line. Each *Mutzav* was invariably on high ground with wide fields of view to allow constant observation of Syrian dispositions and movements. The *Mutzavim* were not intended as true fighting positions but primarily to direct artillery fire and close air support against any enemy incursion.

Over time, the Syrians adopted a prolonged campaign of harassment by artillery fire coupled with infiltration by infantry units to capture specific Israeli positions in order to inflict debilitating casualties upon the Israeli troops. On occasions, these

Israeli reservists hastily load their Shot Meteor tanks with ammunition and stores soon after the outbreak of the Yom Kippur War. The fate of Israel depended on the speed of mobilization of the IDF reserve armoured formations arriving on the Golan Plateau before the Syrian army captured the Golan Heights and thus threatened Israel proper. (IGPO)

A pair of Shot Meteors stands ready for action with a group of M-3 Half Tracks – note the empty shell cases in the foreground. This is how the brigade headquarters of Brigadier Yanosh Ben-Gal would have appeared during the decisive battle in the northern sector with the HQ vehicles some one to two kilometres behind the frontlines and protected by two or three tanks: the brigade's final reserve force. Ben Gal did in fact conduct the battle from an M113A1 APC. (IGPO)

escalated into full-blown attacks that became known as 'battle days' as they rarely lasted more than 24 hours. To counter such assaults on the *Mutzavim*, the IDF Northern Command that was responsible for the defence of the Golan Heights constructed tank-firing ramps beside the individual strong-points. These firing ramps dominated the surrounding terrain and allowed tanks to engage targets to well beyond 2,000 metres range. A deep anti-tank ditch protected by mines was dug along the Purple Line to deter encroachment by Syrian AFVs but such measures were alien to IDF armoured doctrine that advocated that the best form of defence was offence. In time of war, it was axiomatic that the IDF would take the battle on to enemy territory and field fortifications did not sit comfortably with this strategy.

Following the Six Day War, the IDF had been seduced into the conviction that the tank was the primary weapon of ground warfare, supported by an all-powerful air force that would guarantee air supremacy. With a limited defence budget and the air force taking priority in all expenditure – 52 per cent of the total in 1973, it was impossible to meet all the demands. In the army, the armoured corps took precedence over the other arms and so more tanks were procured at the expense of mechanized infantry vehicles or self-propelled artillery weapons. At the time of the Six Day War there were 338 Centurions in service with the IDF. Many more were purchased on the international arms market – 90 in 1967, 100 in 1968, 120 in 1969, 120 in 1970, 120 in 1971 and 100 in 1972. Armoured brigades were now configured with up to three tank battalions but with no integral mechanized infantry component. A tank battalion comprised three companies with three platoons of three tanks plus two more in company headquarters for a total of 11 in each company. With three tank battalions of 36, a fully organized brigade had 111 tanks including three in brigade HQ. Mechanized infantry was to be allocated depending on the mission within the overall *ugda* or divisional plan.

Facing the Israeli forces deployed on the Golan Plateau was a Syrian standing army of three infantry divisions and two armoured divisions stationed within striking distance of the Purple Line. To the north was the 7th Infantry Division deployed from the foothills of Mount Hermon to Kuneitra where it linked up with the 9th Infantry Division that in turn linked up with the 5th Infantry Division at Rafid. These were infantry divisions in name only since each was composed of two infantry brigades, each with an integral tank battalion of T-54/55 tanks, together with one mechanized and one armoured brigade. There were therefore 180 T-54/55 tanks in each infantry division while the armoured divisions were each equipped with 230 of the more modern T-62 tanks armed with the 115mm smoothbore gun. In addition, there were 400 T-54/55s in independent armoured brigades to give a grand total of 1,400 tanks. These were supported by 115 batteries of artillery ranging from 85mm to 203mm, with a total of 950 guns with 70 to 80 guns per kilometre at the designated breakthrough points. Although impressive by any standards, this was still only half that stipulated by Soviet doctrine. The Syrian strategy was to attack in overwhelming force and recapture the Golan Plateau within 36 hours, as this was the time thought to be available before the Israeli reserves could be mobilized. Time was therefore of the essence for both sides. The Syrians had to complete their offensive before the reserves were deployed on to the Golan Heights while the Israelis had to fight a delaying action long enough for the reserves to be mobilized.

In the autumn of 1973 there was just one armoured brigade deployed on the Golan Plateau, facing some 1,400 tanks. The 188th Barak Armored Brigade – Barak is Hebrew for Lightning – was a regular formation of two tank battalions with just 69 Shot Cal Upgraded Centurions. It was an absurd disparity of forces but the Israelis were the victims of their own hubris. Since the end of the War of Attrition, Israeli military intelligence, AMAN, was convinced that Egypt would not go to war until such time as its air force was a match for the Israeli Air Force and that would not be

A trio of Shot Cals manoeuvres in dead ground to avoid observation from the enemy and the devastating effects of the Syrian artillery bombardments. During the initial offensive, the Syrian artillery barrage was so intense that it was nigh on impossible for the Israeli supply trucks to reach the frontlines with ammunition. Accordingly, Jeeps and half-tracks had to retrieve ammunition from knocked-out tanks while under enemy fire, in order to resupply those still fighting. (IGPO)

Fitters of the IDF Ordnance Corps replace the damaged idler wheel of a Shot Cal while an engine change takes place in the background. It cannot be overstated how important the contribution of the Ordnance Corps was in the final victory on the Golan, particularly in the opening Syrian offensive when the repair of damaged tanks was often critical before the arrival of reserve formations. The fitters worked around the clock to refurbish and repair tanks and return them to the frontlines as rapidly as possible whereas the Syrian army made virtually no attempts to recover and repair tank casualties: there were always new ones to replaced those knocked out in battle. (IGPO)

until 1975 at the earliest. Furthermore, Syria would not fight Israel without Egypt and therefore there was no possibility of all-out war for the foreseeable future. It was a concept born of arrogance and an abiding contempt for the fighting abilities of the Arab armies, particularly Syria. Accordingly, the IDF high command remained unconcerned that the force ratio on the Golan Heights was approximately 20:1 since some 70 Shot Cal tanks were deemed sufficient to deal with any 'battle day' given there was no real chance of war. Even in the most unlikely of circumstances that major hostilities broke out, AMAN had promised that it would provide at least 48 hours warning: more than enough time to mobilize the reserves. Anyway the Israeli Air Force was on hand to support the ground forces and stem any assault from the outset.

On 13 September 1973, Israeli F-4E and Mirage IIICJ fighters were escorting a photoreconnaissance mission by RF-4E Phantoms tracking Soviet arms shipments to the port of Tartous. Syrian MiG-21 fighters were scrambled to intercept them but in the ensuing aerial combat 13 Syrian aircraft were shot down with just one Israeli loss. It was the pretext that allowed the Syrians to move their forces forward and adopt an offensive posture, which the Israelis interpreted as purely a public response to the catastrophic air battle. However, it prompted Minister of Defense Moshe Dayan to visit the Golan Heights on 25 September, together with General Eli Zeira, the head of AMAN, and inspect the Israeli defences. On a tour of the frontlines, he was briefed by Major Shmuel Askarov, the deputy commander of the 53rd Tank Battalion of the Barak Brigade. At just 24, Askarov was the youngest deputy battalion commander in the army with a rising reputation. He stated unequivocally: 'War is certain.' Dayan turned to Zeira for his comments only to be told blandly that there would not be a war for another ten years.

Nevertheless, after consultation with Major General Yitzhak 'Khaka' Hofi, the GOC Northern Command, Dayan authorized the deployment of a single tank battalion of the famed 7th Armored Brigade from its base at Beersheba in the Negev Desert to the Golan Heights as reinforcement to the Barak Brigade. The 77th 'Oz' Tank Battalion travelled northwards on the eve of Rosh Hashana, the Jewish New Year, and was equipped with Shot Cals held in reserve by Northern Command. By 1 October, the battalion under the command of a dynamic Yemenite, Lieutenant Colonel Avigdor Khalani, was deployed on the Golan Heights with 22 tanks: the odds were now 15:1. General Hofi was now thoroughly alarmed by the Syrian build-up and he ordered that the anti-tank ditches be widened and deepened as well as the sowing of thousands more mines and for further tank firing ramps to be created on the hill features of Hermonit and Booster Ridge that dominated the Kuneitra Gap. It was here that Northern Command believed the Syrians would launch their main offensive if war broke out, as it would give them the shortest axis of advance to the main Israeli military base and headquarters on the Golan at Nafakh and from there onwards to the Bnot Ya'akov Bridge across the Jordan River. As a further precaution, Hofi replaced the reserve infantry battalions in the *Mutzavim* with hardened troops of the Golani Brigade in the strong points to the north of Kuneitra and paratroopers of the 50th Parachute Battalion in those to the south.

The Syrian tank crews displayed great determination and considerable courage during their initial offensive. They continued to advance despite fearful casualties and they came within a hair's breadth of victory on Sunday 7 October. These T-54A tanks were reputedly destroyed by the Shot Cals of the 77th 'Oz' Tank Battalion of Lieutenant Colonel Avigdor Kahalani in the area that became known as the Valley of Tears. The Arabic numerals on the nearest tank show the callsign 300. (IGPO)

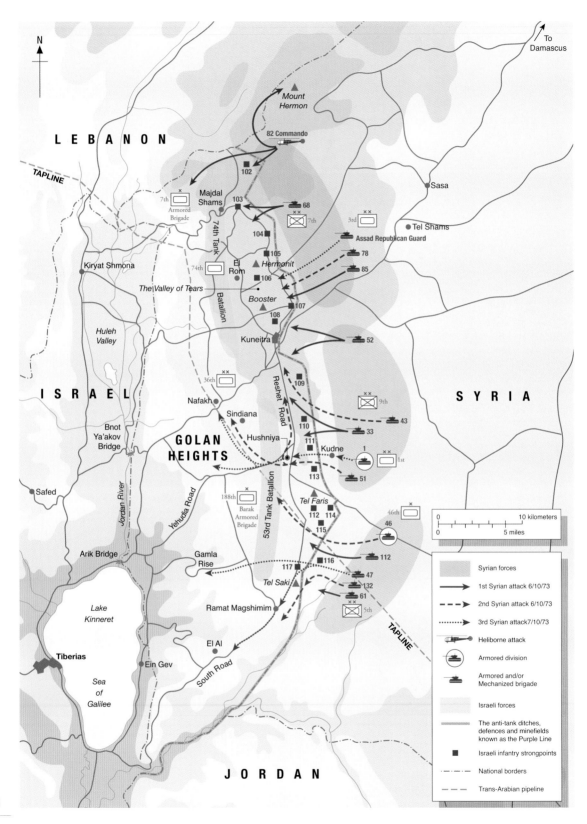

N

To
Damascus

LEBANON

TAPLINE

Mount
Hermon

82 Commando

102

Majdal
Shams

7th
Armored
Brigade

103

68

7th

3rd

Sasa

Tel Shams

Assad Republican Guard

104

74th Tank

105

Hermonit

78

El
Rom

106

85

Kiryat Shmona

74th

The Valley of Tears

Booster

Battalion

108

107

Kuneitra

52

Huleh
Valley

ISRAEL

SYRIA

109

Nafakh

36th

110

9th

43

Sindiana

33

Reshet Road

111

Kudne

1

1st

GOLAN
HEIGHTS

Hushniya

Bnot
Ya'akov
Bridge

113

51

Safed

188th
Barak
Armored
Brigade

Tel Faris

112 114

46th

115

46

Jordan River

53rd Tank Battalion

Yehudia Road

Arik Bridge

Gamla
Rise

116

112

117

47

Tel Saki

132

61

Lake
Kinneret

Ramat Magshimim

5th

TAPLINE

Tiberias

El Al

Sea
of
Galilee

Ein Gev

South Road

JORDAN

0						10 kilometers

0   5 miles

Syrian forces

1st Syrian attack 6/10/73

2nd Syrian attack 6/10/73

3rd Syrian attack7/10/73

Heliborne attack

Armored division

Armored and/or
Mechanized brigade

Israeli forces

The anti-tank ditches,
defences and minefields
known as the Purple Line

Israeli infantry strongpoints

National borders

Trans-Arabian pipeline

50

The Syrians were well aware of the dispositions of the Israeli forces on the Golan Plateau and made their plans accordingly, with the help of their numerous Soviet advisors. While the 7th Division was to tie down the Israel forces to the north of Kuneitra, the main attack was to be made by the 9th Division through the Kudne Gap via Hushniya to Nafakh and on to the Jordan River. Meanwhile, the 5th Division was to break through the Rafid Gap and exploit southwestwards down the South Road to El Al blocking any Israeli reinforcements climbing up the escarpment from the Sea of Galilee. Waiting in the wings were the powerful 1st and 3rd Armoured Divisions, ready to exploit any success with their potent T-62s and brand new BMP-1 Mechanized Infantry Combat Vehicles. This formidable force was supported by a vast array of artillery weapons including FROG ground-to-ground rockets capable of striking Israeli population centres. Helicopter-borne commandos were poised to land deep behind Israeli lines to capture key crossroads and choke points in order to disrupt supplies or reinforcements from reaching the frontline units. Like the Egyptians along the Suez Canal, the Syrians now believed they had the answer to the fearsome Israeli Air Force in the shape of the innovative SA-6 Gainful anti-aircraft missile system combined with the highly mobile ZSU-23-4 Shilka self-propelled anti-aircraft gun. The plan was well conceived and had every chance of success given the complacency of the enemy. The scene was set for an armoured battle of epic proportions.

The speed of the IDF mobilization on Yom Kippur was a major factor in the successful defence of the Golan Plateau, where Syrian plans were based on the first Israeli reserves being deployed in 24 hours whereas the first reserve tanks arrived at Nafakh around 2100 hours, just seven hours after the war began. (IGPO)

A pair of T-55s and a BMP-1 Infantry Fighting Vehicle lie abandoned on the Golan Heights where some 867 Syrian tanks were lost in the fighting out of a total force of 1,400. Many intact T-54/55 tanks were captured by the Israelis and they were modified for service with the Israeli Armored Corps as the Tiran. According to Israeli sources, no BMP-1s managed to cross the Purple Line in the northern sector so this suggests these vehicles were lost to the 188th Barak Brigade. (United Nations)

COUNTDOWN TO WAR

The Israeli forces on the Golan Plateau were part of the 36th Armored Division under the command of Major General Rafael 'Raful' Eitan, with his headquarters at Nafakh. In the opening days of October, they remained wholly inadequate in face of the threat. On Friday 5 October, the IDF Chief of Staff Lieutenant General David Elazar ordered a Gimel alert that cancelled all leave and warned staff officers to prepare for the immediate mobilization of reservists. The personnel of the other two tank battalions of the 7th Armored Brigade, the 71st and 83rd, were flown north and rapidly equipped with Shot Cal tanks before joining the 77th on the Golan Heights. The 7th Armored Brigade was the most prestigious armoured formation in the IDF, having been formed during the War of Independence. The brigade was commanded by Colonel Avigdor 'Yanosh' Ben-Gal, a lanky 38-year old who had risen through the ranks of the IAC. When his family was killed in the Holocaust, Ben-Gal arrived in Palestine in 1944 from Poland via Siberia, India, Teheran and Egypt: in his own words: 'I joined the army in 1955. The army was my home. I was born again. My second birth was in a tank.' Despite his unkempt appearance, he was a consummate professional soldier and a skilled proponent of armoured warfare. His battalion commanders were similarly highly experienced, with Lieutenant Colonel Meshulam Rattes as OC 71st Tank Battalion and Lieutenant Colonel Haim Barak, OC 82nd Tank Battalion. The brigade also included a Sayeret reconnaissance unit mostly mounted in Jeeps and Armoured Personnel Carriers (APC). In addition, the 75th Armored Infantry Battalion commanded by Lieutenant Colonel Yos Eldar was attached to the brigade with their M-113 APCs and M-3 Half Tracks.

In time of war, the 7th Armored Brigade was part of Southern Command and deputed to lead any counter-offensive across the Suez Canal. To this end, one of its tank companies of the 82nd was assigned the specialized role of towing bridging equipment across the desert to prepared crossing points on the banks of the Suez Canal. But even before Minister of Defense Moshe Dayan had ordered the 77th to the northern front, Colonel Ben-Gal had had a premonition of the prospect of war on the Golan Heights. On 23 September, he organized a familiarization tour of the Golan Heights for his brigade staff and battalion commanders. Their newfound knowledge of the difficult terrain was to be of inestimable value in the forthcoming battles. Days of frantic preparation followed as the other battalions of the 7th Armored Brigade requisitioned tanks and equipment from the depots of Northern Command before deploying on to the Golan Heights. The Shot Cals were taken out of storage, tested and loaded with ammunition and equipment before the guns were zeroed. Meanwhile, company and platoon commanders were criss-crossing the Golan Heights to familiarize themselves further with the terrain. Throughout the night of Friday 5 October, tank transporters and supply trucks groaned up the escarpment to the Golan Heights including large stocks of ammunition. Northern Command had authorized an extra 200 rounds per tank as well as more 155mm shells for the 11 batteries of M-109 Self-Propelled Howitzers: just 45 guns as against the 930 of the Syrians but it was the only M-109 regiment in service. The 7th Armored Brigade was directed to complete its deployment to its assembly positions on the Golan Heights by noon on 6 October 1973, the Day of Atonement or Yom Kippur. There were now 177 Shot Cals in place on the Golan Heights: the odds were down to 8:1.

Yom Kippur was the day chosen for the simultaneous offensive by Egypt and Syria against Israel. It is the holiest day in the Judaic calendar but the state of the tides in the Suez Canal and the amount of moonlight were more important to the Egyptians while Syria wished to attack before the winter snows arrived. Egypt was determined to break the diplomatic logjam in order to reclaim the Sinai Peninsula while Syria sought to regain the Golan Heights by force of arms. The Arab armies fielded some 4,480 tanks and AFVs with 4,300 APCs while Israel possessed 2,000 tanks and 4,000 APCs. Almost all were committed to battle in the Sinai Peninsula and on the Golan

At the forefront of the Syrian offensive at the outbreak of the Yom Kippur War were special-purpose variants of the T-55 whose task was to breach the Israeli anti-tank defences along the Purple Line. This T-55 is fitted with a KMT-5 mine-roller and integral mine plough. The system weighs 7.5 tonnes and can be operated at 12–18km/h depending on terrain and soil conditions. Such vehicles were priority targets to Israeli gunners. (United Nations)

53

The anti-tank defences along the Purple Line proved crucial in stalling the Syrian offensive for sufficient time to allow the reserve units to reach the Golan. The anti-tank ditch was five metres across and three metres deep with the spoil heaped up on the Israeli side to make bridgelaying operations more difficult. Anti-tank mines were laid on each side of the ditch and a maintenance road ran along the Israeli side. Such an obstacle is only effective if covered by fire and the IDF constructed a series of firing ramps on higher ground some 1,500 to 2,000 metres to the west of the ditch. From these dominating positions, the Shot Cals were in hull-down positions with just their gun and turret tops showing that made them extremely difficult targets from the front. They in turn were able to engage and destroy Syrian tanks out to a distance of 3,000 metres, such as these ones with a group of T-62As and BTR-152 APCs in the foreground, a T-54A in the ditch and a T-55A(M) toppled off the bridge of an MTU-20. Note how the ditch has been levelled by Caterpillar bulldozers that breached the anti-tank ditch under the cover of darkness. This part of the Purple Line was in the northern sector of the 7th Armored Brigade. (IGPO)

Heights. The total number of AFVs was greater than those at the battle of Kursk and they fought in a smaller geographical area than the Kursk salient. With separate but simultaneous attacks from north and south, the parallels between the two offensives were remarkable. At 1345 hours, Israeli observers on Mount Hermon noticed the camouflage netting being removed from the hundreds of Syrian gun positions on the Damascus Plain. At 1356 hours, a thunderous artillery barrage fell upon the Israeli positions on the Golan Plateau that lasted 50 minutes without pause. Simultaneously, MiG-19 ground attack aircraft swooped down to bomb and strafe the headquarters at Nafakh. At that precise moment, Colonel Ben-Gal was giving his last-minute briefing to his battalion commanders and their company commanders at the base. He immediately gave a single, simple order: 'Everyone to your tanks!'

LIGHTNING STRIKES

At that moment, Major Shmuel Askarov, the deputy commander of the 53rd Tank Battalion, was in his office at the Hushniya base of the 188th Barak Brigade. His Shot Cal was parked outside his door with the crew within hailing distance. As he had indicated to General Moshe Dayan ten days earlier, he was certain that war was imminent. Throughout the night, the command elements of the brigade had been in conference revising plans and preparations. The commander of the 188th Barak Brigade was the Turkish-born Colonel Yitzhak Ben-Shoham. The brigade was composed of just two battalions with the 74th Tank Battalion commanded by Lieutenant Colonel Yair Nafshi deployed in the north from the slopes of Mount Hermon to near Mutzva 109 to the south of Kuneitra and the 53rd Tank Battalion commanded by Lieutenant Colonel Oded Erez from Mutzva 109 southwards. There were just 69 Shot Cals scattered along some 43 miles of front bordering the Purple Line giving an average of one and a half tanks per mile of front. Nevertheless, Ben-Shoham had received no indication from Generals Hofi or Eitan that the Syrians were likely to launch anything besides another 'battle day'. The radio net of the brigade was designated 'Toffee' and it immediately despatched the codeword – 'Capital'. It was the signal for the tanks of the brigade to move to their assigned positions on the firing ramps beside the various *Mutzavim*. Major Askarov was in his tank within moments and heading eastwards at high speed through the heavy artillery barrage to Mutzav 111 overlooking the Kudne Gap. As his Shot Cal mounted the firing ramp he could see nothing but churning clouds of dust due to the intensive shelling. Eventually, there was a lull and the dust settled momentarily. He was dumbfounded when he saw hundreds of Syrian T-54 and T-55 tanks emerging from the dust cloud in dense columns spearheaded by specialized bridge-laying and mine-clearing variants.

All along the Purple Line, the tank platoons of the Barak Brigade were under fire as they manoeuvred into their pre-assigned firing positions. In the northern sector, the 74th Tank Battalion was deployed with Company Het under the command of Captain Eyal Shaham with its three platoons guarding Mutzavim 104, 105 and 107 with the company commander and two tanks at Mas'adeh. Company Alef under the command of Major Zvi Rak was stationed in and around Kuneitra as it was thought to be a Syrian priority objective for a 'battle day'. Company Bet under the command of Major Avner Landau was held in reserve at Wasset Junction, while the battalion commander Lieutenant Colonel Nafshi stationed himself on the commanding heights of Booster Ridge overlooking the Kuneitra Gap. At 1415 hours, an observation post on Hermonit reported the advance of an armoured force of T-54/55s proceeded by bridging and mine-clearing tanks but Nafshi immediately implemented a coordinated fire plan of tanks and artillery that stopped the enemy before they reached the anti-tank ditch. But the pressure was mounting by the minute. The Syrian 68th Infantry Brigade with an attached tank battalion of T-54/55s launched an assault between Mutzavim 104 and 105 but Nafshi promptly despatched Company Bet to the threatened area and caught the enemy in the flank as the MTU-20s were trying to deploy their bridges over the anti-tank ditch. A further attack by the Syrian 85th Infantry Brigade to the north and south of *Mutzav* 107 was similarly halted by the 74th as was an attack by the Syrian 52nd Infantry Brigade to the north of Mutzav 109. The Shot Cals on the firing ramps were exacting a fearful toll of the swarming enemy T-54s and T-55s while the few mobile reserves moved from one threatened point of penetration to another. The general feeling at the outset was that this was just another 'battle day' but now the frontline units were reporting that yet more tanks were approaching. Equally serious was that the Shot Cals were running short of ammunition. Even now they were obliged to retire so that the crews could access the rounds hidden in the bowels of the tanks.

South of Mutzav 109, the 53rd Tank Battalion was under even more intense pressure as the 5th and 9th Infantry Divisions mounted the main Syrian attacks through the Kudne and Rafid Gaps. Company Zayin under the command of Captain

Uri Avika was deployed from Mutzav 110 to 114, together with Major Askarov, covering the Kudne line. Immediately to their south was Company Gimmel under the command of Captain Uzi Arieli, although three tanks of his tanks were detached to protect brigade HQ. The company's task was to guard the Tapline Road with a platoon of tanks at Juhader close to Mutzavim 114 and 115. The Trans Arabian Pipeline or Tapline extended some 1,200 miles from Arabia to the Mediterranean coast in Lebanon and ran diagonally across the Golan. It was to prove crucial in the campaign. As soon as the attack began, reports came in of a Syrian probe along the road bordering the Tapline and Captain Arieli despatched a platoon as reinforcements commanded by Lieutenant Oded Beckman. On arrival at Mutzav 115, his defending force numbered just five Shot Cals. To his front was a Syrian tank battalion of 41 T-54/55s of the 112nd Infantry Brigade giving a ratio of 1:8. Although his limbs seemed to be shaking uncontrollably, Beckman's mind was crystal clear. He noticed an MTU-20 bridgelayer at the head of the column and allowed it to lay its bridge across the anti-tank ditch and withdraw. Only when a T-54 gun tank manoeuvred on to the bridge did he open fire when it was halfway across. He destroyed a second T-54 as it tried to push aside the first one, effectively blocking the crossing site entirely. He then engaged a second MTU-20 before it reached the anti-tank ditch, stalling the whole Syrian attack. All along the Purple Line, the specialized T-54/55 variants of the MTU-20 bridgelayer and the mineclearing PT-54s fitted with mine-rollers were the priority targets to Israeli gunners since their primary role was to breach the anti-tank ditch and the minefields. Standard operating procedure dictated that these vehicles were engaged at the maximum effective range of 2,500 metres.

Finally, there was Company Vav under the command of Captain Avi Ronis with five tanks near Tel Juhader, a platoon at Mutzav 114 and a platoon under the command of Lieutenant Yoav Yakir at Mutzav 116, the most southern post on the Purple Line. Its role was to block both the Tapline Road and the South Road to El Al. In the more open rolling terrain of the southern Golan Plateau, this was an impossible task for so few tanks.

THE STAND OF THE BARAK BRIGADE

At the command headquarters at Nafakh, confusion reigned since many of the senior officers were absent including General Khaka Hofi, his deputy, chief of staff and the commander of the resident 36th Armored Division, Major General Raful Eitan. At noon, Hofi had flown to Tel Aviv in his Piper Cub leaving Colonel Ben-Shoham in command of the Golan: a fact he failed to convey to Colonel Ben-Gal. Accordingly, the latter baulked at being given orders by his equivalent in rank to move two of his battalions to the Wasset Junction. He returned to Nafakh to clarify the situation only to find the command bunker jammed packed with personnel sheltering from the artillery bombardment. Finding it impossible to talk to Ben-Shoham, he informed the Northern Command operations officer, Lieutenant Colonel Uri Simhoni, that he was going to move the 7th Armored Brigade towards Kuneitra. Ben-Shoham himself was frantically busy communicating with his two battalion commanders as they fought their desperate battles along the Purple Line. Realizing the problem in the chain of command, Shimoni took it upon himself to assume the authority of the GOC Northern Command. Thus, a mere lieutenant colonel assumed command in the opening hours of Israel's most critical battle. Crucially, both the full colonels, Ben-Gal and Ben-Shoham, were willing to take orders from a subordinate in rank as the representative of Northern Command.

Shimoni's first decision was to have far-reaching consequences and effectively set the course of the battle for the next four days. Within the first hour of battle being joined, he ordered Ben-Gal to move two of his battalions to the sector north of Kuneitra and one to the southern Golan. The tanks moved out of their assembly points around Nafakh and headed eastwards along the various tracks and roadways but still carefully trying to avoid running over the irrigation pipes of the Golan kibbutz farmers. Under withering artillery fire, the 7th Armored Brigade deployed along the high ground some two and a half miles from the Purple Line, acting as an immediate reserve to the Barak Brigade now heavily engaged along the whole of the 43-mile frontlines, giving an average of just one and a half tanks per mile of front. This meant there were to be three tank battalions north of Kuneitra and two to the south. His decision was based on the information he was receiving from the front. The 53rd Tank Battalion's initial reports indicated that they were containing the Syrian attacks in the southern sector. But in the north the observation posts on lofty Mount Herman and the tall *tels* were able to see the magnitude of the overall offensive from their elevated positions, a facility denied to the 53rd. It also reinforced the mindset of Northern Command that was convinced that the Syrians would attack through the Kuneitra Gap following repeated wargames by the Israelis. Critically at this juncture, there were no more reserves to be had as the general mobilization of the IDF had only just been set in motion. Yet, with no intelligence to the contrary, Colonel Ben-Shoham was still convinced that this was just another 'battle day' whereas Ben-Gal realized this was general warfare on two fronts. By mid-afternoon, Ben-Gal decided to visit the frontlines to see for himself and organize his brigade accordingly while Ben-Shoham remained in the command bunker at Nafakh and directed his brigade by radio.

At Mutzav 111, the deputy commander of the Barak Brigade was perched on a firing ramp in his Shot Cal opposite the Syrian fortification on Tel Kudne. To his front, the ground was still shrouded in dust and smoke as the Syrian artillery bombardment continued unabated. When the barrage lifted, Major Shmuel Askarov saw scores of tanks pressing forward in columns four abreast astride the Kudne Road as the 33rd Infantry Brigade launched its assault. Five MTU-20 bridgelayers were in the van. In his crew, Askarov had the finest gunner in the brigade, Yitzhak Hemo. Within minutes, three of the bridgelayers were in flames but Askarov suddenly realized that he was fighting alone. His accompanying tanks were sheltering behind the ramps from the fearsome artillery fire. Askarov immediately called up his fellow tank commanders by radio but got little response. Ordering his driver to reverse, he drew up beside the closest Shot Cal and jumped across. Drawing his pistol he pointed it at

OVERLEAF
On the night of 6 October and long into the next day, Lieutenant Zvi 'Zvika' Greengold fought one of the most remarkable individual tank battles in the annals of armoured warfare. Unattached to any particular unit as he was on a company commander's course at the Armored School, he hitchhiked to Nafakh at the outbreak of war where he took command a pair of Shot Cals and set off down the Tapline Road at 2100 hours in the dark with absolutely no knowledge of the whereabouts of the enemy. For the next 20 hours using the callsign 'Force Zvika' to disguise the size of his unit, he fought to stem the advance of the Syrian 51st Armoured Brigade, mainly on his own but occasionally with other tanks. Singlehandedly, he destroyed some 40 Syrian tanks but claims only 20 while having to change tanks six times due to battle damage. Although wounded, he fought on and disrupted the final Syrian assault on the IDF headquarters at Nafakh. Burnt and bloodied, the 21-year old Lt Zvi 'Zvika' Greengold finally climbed down from his Shot Cal and collapsed saying simply – 'I can't anymore.' For his extraordinary gallantry, Lt Zvi Greengold was awarded the Medal of Valor.

Zvi 'Zvika' Greengold receives the Medal Of Valor on 8 May 1975 from the President of Israel, Efraim Katzir, with Defense Minister Shimon Peres to the President's right and Prime Minister Yitzhak Rabin to his left. Lieutenant Greengold was just 21 when he fought his heroic action on the Tapline Road against the Syrian 51st Armoured Brigade as part of Force Zvika. He later rose to the rank of major in the reserves and became the director general of Israel Oil Refineries. He is currently the mayor of Ofakim in the Negev Desert. (IGPO)

the commander's head and ordered 'Get up there or I shoot', indicating the firing ramps. The other tanks quickly mounted the ramps and began firing methodically up and down the long lines of T-54/55s but still they kept advancing. With a display of cold courage not seen before by the Israelis, the Syrian tanks simply bypassed the burning victims of the devastating Israeli fire and pressed on, pausing occasionally to return fire.

Where the terrain permitted, groups detached themselves from the advancing columns and engaged the Shot Cals on the ramps with volley after volley of armour-piercing shot, despite the difficulty of hitting such small targets. Inevitably, rounds struck home and one by one the tanks on the ramps were hit and most of their commanders killed, since the Israeli commanders fought with the heads outside of the cupolas for better vision. Askarov's Shot Cal was hit four times but remained operational. Within the first two hours, his crew destroyed 35 T-54/55s and numerous APCs, thanks to the superb gunnery of Yitzhak Hemo, who achieved a remarkable hit rate of one enemy AFV for every one and half rounds fired. Each Shot Cal carried 72 rounds. But still the Syrians advanced and closed on the ramps. Soon after 1600 hours, Hemo hit a tank to the left of his ramp at a range of just 50 yards but by now there were others even closer. Akarov swung the turret to the right to allow Hemo to engage another T-54 at 30 yards range but the two tanks fired simultaneously. Askarov was blown out of his commander's cupola with serious wounds to the throat and head. As dusk fell, the Kudne Road was now open.

To the north of Kuneitra, the fighting was bitter and intense around Mutzav 107 as the Syrian 52nd Infantry Brigade attacked in force with scores of tanks along the Damascus Road. Facing them were just the three Shot Cals of Lieutenant Shmuel Yakhin's platoon of Company Alef, 74th Tank Battalion. The three tanks were perched on the firing ramps several hundred yards apart on each side of the strongpoint that was manned by men of the 1st Golani Infantry Brigade. They opened fire at 2,000 yards' range inflicting numerous casualties among the enemy. Volley after volley of APDS rounds crashed into the advancing AFVs until the ammunition ran low. The company commander, Major Zvi Rak, arrived with seven tanks to add their firepower to Yakhin's platoon. Burning wrecks and exploding vehicles now dotted the landscape until the column veered to the south and out of range. Major Rak sent his deputy, Captain Oded Yisraeli, with a platoon of tanks in pursuit. He soon discovered a company of T-54/55s crossing the anti-tank ditch over a bridge laid by an MTU-20. The enemy were lined up like ducks at a fairground and all the tanks were destroyed within minutes. A mile further on, Yisraeli encountered another company attempting to cross but the Syrian tanks returned fire with determination. Syrian combat engineers had found the answer to the anti-tank ditch and were now filling it in with an unarmoured Caterpillar bulldozer. Captain Yisraeli called his company commander for reinforcements. Leaving Yakhin's platoon at Mutzav 107, Major Rak and his four tanks moved southwards in support but he suddenly heard an explosion and found himself covered in blood. It took some moments before he realized it was not his own but that of his loader, who had been decapitated by an Rocket Propelled Grenade (RPG). His headless torso slumped down into the turret spurting arterial blood around the interior. Both the gunner and driver became hysterical at the sight of their comrade's body. Rak slapped them and doused them in water until they calmed down. He then returned to Kuneitra to extricate the body and change to another Shot Cal. Such deaths occurred regularly during the first few days of the campaign. Although it was a relatively simple matter for Ordnance Corps personnel to clean the interior of the turret of blood, it did not take long it for the residue to become malodorous, much to the discomfort of subsequent crews. The answer was found by wiping the interior walls of the turret with diesel oil as its smell masked the stench of the blood or decaying flesh. Furthermore, so many tank crewmen, especially tank commanders, were being decapitated that crews were ordered to wear their dog tags around their ankles since they were often lost from a headless body.

Far to the south, a platoon of Company Vav under the command of Lieutenant Yoav Yakir had been fighting a lone action all afternoon. Although assigned to support the southernmost strongpoint of Mutzav 116, he had fought an action near Tel Saki against a force of some 25 T-54/55s trying to cross the Purple Line along an old Roman road that once led to Damascus. Together with his first sergeant Nir Atir, Yakir destroyed most of them by accurate, long-range tank fire. Around 1600 hours, the Syrian 47th Tank Brigade attached to the 5th Infantry Division was observed advancing on the anti-tank ditch opposite Mutzav 116. The strongpoint's commander, 2nd Lieutenant Yossi Gur of the 50th Parachute Battalion, immediately radioed to Lieutenant Yakir for support as his position was being blanketed in artillery fire. Yakir's platoon hurried north to Mutzav 116 where the Syrians had deployed bridges across the anti-tank ditch and tanks were streaming across. The three Shot Cals engaged the 60 T-55s of the 47th Tank Brigade from open terrain at ranges from 200 to 1,000 yards. They were joined by two tanks from a neighbouring platoon but these were soon knocked out: the gallant platoon was once more fighting alone. As darkness fell, they fought on by the light of flares fired from Mutzav 116 until 2300 hours by when two of Yakir's tanks had fired all their ammunition and the other had just five rounds left. Lieutenant Yakhir sought permission to withdraw and be resupplied with ammunition but the situation was so desperate that he was ordered to continue the action with just machine-gun fire to try and dissuade the Syrians from advancing in the dark. A few minutes later, Yakir was killed and Sergeant Nir Atir assumed command of the platoon. Realizing the hopelessness of the situation, Colonel Ben-Shoham ordered Atir to withdraw for more ammunition. The platoon had been fighting for seven hours without respite but, just as it fell back, the very first reinforcements were finally arriving on the Golan Heights, albeit just ten tanks of a ready reaction battalion. The Barak Brigade and its 69 Shot Cals had destroyed scores of Syrian T-54/55s and numerous other AFVs but the battle was to continue long into the night.

7TH BRIGADE ENTERS THE FRAY

Major General Khaka Hofi arrived at the Nafakh headquarters at 1630 hours in company with Major General Mordechai 'Motti' Hod, the former head of the Israeli Air Force and the architect of the pre-emptive strike in the Six Day War of 1967: a stratagem denied to the IDF in October 1973 by the government. He immediately concurred with Colonel Shimoni's disposition of forces but he divided the front into two separate commands. The 7th Armored Brigade was to assume responsibility for the northern sector and absorb the remnants of the 74th Tank Battalion into its command. The southern sector was now the responsibility of the 188th Barak Brigade, comprising its own 53rd Tank Battalion and the 82nd Tank Battalion, transferred in from the 7th Armored Brigade. The latter was now deployed along the high ground some two miles behind the frontlines with the 71st Tank Battalion in the north, and the 77th Tank Battalion in the centre covering the Kuneitra Gap from the hill feature of Booster down to the deserted town of Kuneitra itself. Between them was the 75th Armored Infantry Battalion, reinforced by Company Humous under Lieutenant Emi Palant from the 77th Tank Battalion. The 82nd Tank Battalion had moved south to support the 188th Armored Brigade and was now positioned in reserve but unfortunately Lieutenant Colonel Oded Erez had not been informed of their presence. During the afternoon's fighting, the 53rd had lost 12 tanks, a third of its total. Two company commanders had been killed and the battalion deputy commander, Major Shmuel Askarov, wounded. He was now in hospital at Safed. Following an operation on his throat and for his other injuries, he was told he must remain in hospital for at least two weeks to recover. The 74th in the north had lost seven of its 33 tanks but had contained every Syrian attack so far. The crews were exhausted by their exertions and the fearful concussion of exploding artillery shells. Although the crews were relatively immune inside their tanks to artillery fire, the red-hot fragments sheared off radio antennae, damaged optical sights and ignited camouflage nets or bedding on the exteriors rendering the vehicles deaf and blind until repairs could be made. Such artillery fire was also deadly to crew commanders standing with their head and shoulders exposed in their cupolas for better vision of the battlefield.

Around 1700 hours as dusk fell, the Syrians resumed the offensive with major attacks by a further two brigades in the northern sector and three more in the south against the hard-pressed Barak Brigade. Thanks to the intelligence gained during previous 'battle days', the Syrians knew the dispositions of all the *Mutzavim* and the firing ramps. In the failing light, tanks and infantry infiltrated through the gaps in the Israeli defences in large numbers. Infantry tank hunter teams now moved among the frontline positions. T-54s and T-55s were pouring through the Israeli lines in the southern sector with approximately 140 in the Kudne area, some 60 advancing along the Tapline Road towards Hushniya and another 150 breaking through around Mutzavim 115 and 116. The 53rd Tank Battalion had just 15 tanks left fighting these hordes of T-54/55s along the Purple Line. The Syrians were now exerting intense pressure along the entire Israeli defence line from Mount Hermon to Tel Saki.

A formation of Shot Cals moves forward into Syria showing the revised rear hull and engine decks of the upgraded model together with the air filter boxes on the trackguards. (IGPO)

The 53rd was desperately low on ammunition but it was virtually impossible to withdraw and reload since the Syrians would have quickly overrun the firing ramps. Lieutenant Colonel Erez radioed for more supplies to be brought forward. At 1830 hours, Colonel Ben-Shoham decided to leave Nafakh and join his brigade. In his M-3 Half Track command vehicle, he took with him his operations officer, Major Benny Katzin, while his deputy Lieutenant Colonel David Israeli, remained at Nafakh but as it neared Hushniya it came under such intense artillery fire that Ben-Shoham radioed for his Shot Cal be brought to him. When it arrived, the crew informed him that they had passed many tanks in the darkness. Since the Barak Brigade was fighting along the Purple Line some four miles further east, the realization began to dawn on Ben-Shoham that the Syrians must have broken through in force. Belatedly, the 82nd Tank Battalion of Lieutenant Colonel Haim Barak was ordered forward to support the remnants of the Barak Brigade. The 82nd was composed of three companies of which two were made up of recent conscripts only halfway through their basic armour training course. On the other hand, Company Alef commanded by Captain Eli Geva was a veteran unit and considered among the best in the IAC. Company Bet under the command of Captain Yaacov Chessner was despatched to the Kudne sector at Mutzav 111 where it arrived with seven tanks having lost four en route. Company Gimel was sent to support Mutzav 116 but was ambushed on the way, losing seven tanks in its first action. Captain Geva and Company Alef fought a successful battle in the darkness along the patrol road running north–south behind the Purple Line, destroying some 30 tanks for the loss of just one.

The Syrians exploited their success in the south by committing the 1st Armoured Division through the Rafid opening following the successful attack of the 46th Tank Brigade while the 15th Mechanized Brigade of the 3rd Armoured Division expanded the breach in the Israeli line at Kudne. A strong column of AFVs from this formation turned north towards Kuneitra with the intention of striking the southern flank of the 7th Armored Brigade and dislodging it from its dominating fire positions.

All the Syrian tanks from the T-54 to the T-62 of the Syrian armoured divisions were fitted with infrared headlights and projectors to aid night driving and illuminate targets at night with beams of light that were invisible to the human eye without special viewing devices. It gave the Syrians a distinct tactical advantage over the Israelis since their tanks had no such equipment. In the past, night-fighting had been an IDF speciality and they did not believe that the Arabs would continue operations under the cover of darkness. For the same reason, the IDF had too few artillery illuminating rounds and flares as previously the Syrian 'battle days' had invariably ended by nightfall. The failure to equip Israeli forces adequately for night-fighting was to prove costly in the coming hours. Aided by their infrared equipment, Syrian tanks were now infiltrating up the wadis and tracks between the Israeli positions in the northern sector where the Shot Cals of the 74th Tank Battalion had broken the Syrian tanks. Under the cover of darkness, Syrian combat engineers were filling and levelling the anti-tank ditch with bulldozers in numerous places.

Soon after 2100 hours, the renewed Syrian offensive struck the 7th Armored Brigade in the centre at the Hermonit hill feature that was defended by the 75th Armored Infantry Battalion. With clattering tracks and belching diesel exhaust fumes, the Syrian tanks were almost invisible in the dark. The battalion commander Lieutenant Colonel Yos Eldar called for flares to illuminate the battlefield but demands along the front quickly exhausted supplies. It was another glaring tactical and logistical failure by the IDF because they had believed the Syrians usually ended their 'battle days' before nightfall, so flares were deemed unnecessary in large quantities. The Israeli tank crews were now fighting blind. Only some of the tank commanders had special binoculars capable of detecting infrared radiation. On Booster Hill to the south, Lieutenant Colonel Avigdor Kahalani witnessed the Syrian assault and quickly mounted a counterattack. As his tanks approached Hermonit, he heard over the radio that Yos Eldar had been wounded and evacuated so he took command of the battle. It was the first major Syrian incursion across the Purple Line of the day on the 7th Armored Brigade front. With no parachute flares to guide them, the Israeli gunners engaged targets by the light of burning hulks in the valley below. The battle raged for three hours as the Syrian 7th Infantry Division tried repeatedly to overwhelm the 7th Armored Brigade. At one point, Kahalani put his IR-sensitive binoculars to his eyes only to see his own tank bathed in light but when he lowered them he could see nothing. Realizing his tank was being targeted by a T-55 just a few dozen yards away, he ordered his driver, Yuval Ben-Ner, to reverse down the slope immediately. The fighting died down after midnight and the exhausted crews took turns sleeping fitfully not knowing what the morning held.

During the day of Yom Kippur, the Syrians had committed some 720 tanks to battle and despite heavy losses had broken through the Israeli defences in the southern Golan although their timetable was now frustrated and delayed by the gallant defence of the 188th Barak Brigade. Over 300 tanks were now advancing into the heart of the

Golan Plateau. The 132nd Mechanized Brigade was heading southwestwards towards the religious settlement of Ramat Magshimim. The 43rd Tank Brigade began a two-pronged attack with the major thrust towards Nafakh while a secondary force turned northwards up the Reshet Road towards Kuneitra. The last remnants of the Barak Brigade under the command of Lieutenant Colonel Oded Erez were still fighting rearguard actions against appalling odds. Gradually they were forced backwards and the survivors, including three from the 82nd Tank Battalion and three from

the 53rd of Sergeant Atir's platoon that had run out of ammunition, withdrew to the relative safety of Tel Faris where they formed a night leaguer with some paratroopers, support troops and dismounted tank crews. During the night more stragglers arrived but the position was now completely cut off by the Syrians. Worse still, the 51st Tank Brigade with some 100 T-54/55 was now advancing along the Tapline Road towards the Israeli command headquarters at Nafakh and there was not a single Israeli tank in their path. Disaster loomed but was to be averted by the indomitable courage of a solitary lieutenant, Zvi 'Zvika' Greengold. This 21-year-old lieutenant fought for 20 straight hours, changing tanks six times as they were shot out from under him, and is credited with an astonishing 40 enemy tanks, although he himself would claim only 20.

At 0300 hours on 7 October, the column of tanks and AFVs of the 43rd Tank Brigade was spotted moving northwards towards Kuneitra by the tank commander of a disabled Shot Cal. He reported his sighting to Colonel Ben-Gal. The role of the 43rd Tank Brigade was to strike the southern flank of the 7th Armored Brigade and dislodge it from its dominating fire positions. If this attack succeeded, the Israeli defence of the northern Golan would be shattered just as it had been in the south. Ben-Gal immediately ordered his Tiger Company under Captain Meir Zamir to meet the threat. Zamir carefully selected an ambush site with his ten tanks on both sides of the Reshet Road but positioned well back in hulldown positions. Since the Israelis did not possess any night sights on their tanks, they turned off their engines and waited in silence. Soon they heard the rumble of the approaching armoured column. When most of the tanks were in the killing zone, one Shot Cal switched on its searchlight to illuminate the area. Within short order, some 40 T-54/55s were destroyed and the advance northwards halted. While some of the survivors retreated, others turned westwards taking the line of least resistance towards the IDF headquarters at Nafakh.

Around midnight, the full gravity of the situation on the Golan Heights finally began to impinge on the senior officers of Northern Command at Nafakh. Against a background of artillery fire, Generals Hofi and Hod decided to return to the Northern Command headquarters at Safed beyond the Bnot Ya'akov Bridge at 0100 hours after

The lack of a Dushka heavy machine gun at the loader's hatch and no prominent ventilator dome on the turret roof as on the T-54 series indicates that this is a standard production T-55 with a flush hatch for the loader, IR night fighting equipment, D-10T2S 100mm main armament and no hull machine gun. This model also featured an uprated V-55 engine of 580hp, a revolving turret floor, more ammunition and stowage racks at the rear for two 200-litre fuel drums to extend the operating range. (RAC Tank Museum)

AVIGDOR KAHALANI

Avigdor Kahalani was born on 16 June 1944 at Nes Ziona in Palestine to a family of Yemenite extraction. On induction into the IDF, he wished to become a paratrooper but flat feet dictated otherwise and he joined the Israeli Armored Corps in 1962. He was assigned to the 82nd Tank Battalion and served as a gunner on a Centurion tank. After becoming an officer in 1964, he was posted to the Syrian border during the Water War and was then sent to Munsterlager in West Germany to learn about the M48A2C Patton that was being procured by the Israeli Armored Corps. On his return to Israel, he helped to set up the first tank battalion equipped with the Patton within the 7th Armored Brigade.

It was with the 79th Tank Battalion that Kahalani fought in the Six Day War when he was critically wounded during an action at Sheikh Zuweid. His burn injuries were so severe that he was not expected to live but after 16 operations and many months of recuperation he returned to service as an instructor at the Armored Corps School. In 1972, he was sent to the Command and Staff College and then served as deputy commander of the 77th Tank Battalion within the 7th Armored Brigade. In early 1973, Kahalani assumed command of the 77th or 'Oz' Battalion – the number 77 is the numerical equivalent of the Hebrew letters OZ meaning Valour. It was a name he certainly lived up to during the Yom Kippur War during the bitter fighting on the northern sector of the Golan Heights and during the IDF incursion into Syria. For his outstanding courage and leadership during the war, Lieutenant Colonel Avigdor Kahalani was awarded Israel's highest decoration for heroism – Itur HaGvura, or the Medal of Valor. After the war, he became the deputy commander of the Armored Corps School and then took over a reserve training base deep in the Negev Desert. In December 1975, he assumed command of the 7th Armored Brigade as a full colonel. Three years later, he attended the Command and

Lieutenant Colonel Avigdor Kahalani, the commander of the 77th 'Oz' Tank Battalion of the 7th Armored Brigade poses for the camera after a quick shave soon after the decisive battle in the northern sector of the Golan with the Valley of Tears in the background where his comrades in arms destroyed over 500 Syrian AFVs during some 81 hours of intensive combat. For his inspired leadership, Kahalani was awarded the Medal of Valor. (IGPO)

General Staff College at Forth Leavenworth in Kansas, USA. In January 1980, he was promoted to brigadier general and was given command of the 36th Armored Division on the Golan Heights. Nicknamed the Basalt Division because of the rocky terrain of the Golan, it took part in Operation *Peace for Galilee*, the incursion into Lebanon, in June 1982. After the Lebanon campaign, he became the commandant of the Command and Staff College. His final posting in the IDF was as deputy commander of the newly formed Ground Corps Command. On leaving the army, he entered politics and was elected to the Knesset parliament in 1992, later becoming the Minister of Internal Security.

passing command of the Golan to Brigadier General Raful Eitan. Hofi called up IDF Chief of Staff David Elazar and expressed doubts that the Golan Heights could be held but ended by saying that only the Israeli Air Force could stop the Syrians. And for that daylight was necessary. But the air force was committed to a major operation at daybreak against the Egyptian missile screen along the Suez Canal under the codename 'Tagar' that had been in preparation since the War of Attrition. Tagar was cancelled and the air force was ordered north as the present threat to Israel was realized to be measurably greater.

After losing several of their aircraft in the opening hours of the war, the A-4 Skyhawk squadron at Ramat David airbase was now called upon to stem the Syrian armour on the southern Golan. But Syrian SAM-6 missiles quickly found their mark. The ground troops vowed not to call for any further air support. In the first two days of the war, the Israeli Air Force lost 35 aircraft and close air support missions were largely suspended. Despite flying around 500 sorties a day over the Golan, the air force was committed to degrading the Syrian anti-aircraft defences as the priority mission. The reality was the tank platoons and companies were on their own without air support and with only limited artillery assets to stem the Syrian offensive. The deciding factor remained the tank crews themselves and the 105mm guns of their Shot Cals. As one platoon commander later recalled: 'It became clear in the first hour that the battle had been left to the company and platoon commanders and individual tank commanders. The adrenalin rush was tremendous. Orders from some officer in the rear didn't matter much. We were alone and we made the decisions.' No more so was this true than in the epic stand of the 7th Armored Brigade.

IN FIRE THEY WILL COME

At 0400 hours, Lieutenant Colonel Avigdor Kahalani of the 77th Tank Battalion woke in the light of a chilly dawn. Using the callsign 'Shoter' or 'Policeman', he contacted his company commanders and ordered their crews to start their engines. The Shot Cals burst into life and black exhaust smoke filled the air. Some two kilometres to their front scores of T-54/55s were doing the same. It reminded Khahalani of the roar of lions ready to pounce on their prey. He ordered the battalion forward on to the firing ramps overlooking the valley between Hermonit and Booster – the fabled Kuneitra Gap. As the Shot Cals took up their hulldown positions, the Syrians began to advance in serried ranks with all the crew hatches closed. All along the line, the Shot Cals engaged the enemy out to ranges of 1,500 metres; each crew fighting their own private war for survival. Numerous Syrian tanks were hit but the 77th was taking casualties as well. The commander of Vespa Company, Lieutenant Yair Swet, was killed as were seven other tank commanders, mostly from artillery fire as they stood exposed in their cupolas. One Shot Cal was deputed to evacuate the wounded to the medical teams that had moved as close to the front as they could in their vulnerable M-3 Half Tracks. Similarly, the Ordnance Corps Forward Repair Teams were working non-stop to repair any battle-damaged tanks and return them to the fighting troops. But they were inhibited by a lack of armoured recovery vehicles and their half-tracks were not powerful enough to tow the victims so combat engineers on unarmoured bulldozers answered the call despite the devastating enemy artillery bombardment. With grim determination, attack followed attack at 0800 hours; at 0900 hours and again at 1300 hours. Khahalani marvelled at the courage of the Syrians; unseen in previous wars and so all the more unexpected.

The same was not the case in the southern Golan where the 53rd Tank Battalion had just 12 tanks left clustered in a defensive position at Tel Faris. During the night, Colonel Ben-Shoham had been forced back westwards by the relentless Syrian advance. His last order to Oded Erez had been to retire to Tel Faris with the words: 'All we can do now is hang on until the reserves come up. We've done our bit.' At dawn, the first Syrian tanks arrived at Ramat Magshimim. From there, they drove on unopposed towards El Al and halted some 700 yards short. At Mutzav 111, the radio operator intercepted a transmission from the Syrian unit: 'I see the whole Galilee in front of me. Request permission to proceed.' But the request was denied. The opportunity of victory was slipping away as even now the first 25 tanks of Colonel Ran Sarig's 17th Reserve Armored Brigade were crossing the Arik Bridge and climbing the Golan escarpment. The Israeli mobilisation was ahead of schedule. In contrast, the Syrian timetable was falling behind due to the tenacious defence of the Shot Cals. The whole weight of the Syrian offensive was still directed towards Nafakh despite the gallant defence of 'Force Zvika' along the Tapline Road through the night. Col. Ben-Shoman's command team now joined 'Force Zvika'. However, the T-62s of the Syrian 1st Armoured Division were advancing along Yehudia Road threatening to outflank 'Force Zvika' fighting the 51st Tank Brigade on the Tapline Road. On learning of this new threat to his headquarters, Brigadier General Eitan ordered Ben-Shoham to return immediately to Nafakh. With the sun now high in the sky, Ben-Shoham turned his Shot Cal towards Nafakh, standing upright in the turret together with Benny Katzin. As they passed a disabled T-54, they were killed outright by a burst of machine-gun fire. Ben-Shoham's deputy, Lieutenant Colonel David Yisraeli, was also dead, killed in action just moments before. The redoubtable 188th Barak Armored Brigade now ceased to exist.

But its sacrifice had not been in vain as the Centurion tanks of the 679th Reserve Armored Brigade under the command of Colonel Ori Orr was now reaching Nafakh from the west. By nightfall, the attack on Nafakh had been contained but the 1st Armoured Division was still moving inexorably westwards towards the Bnot Ya'ackov Bridge, which was even now being readied for demolition as the Israeli defence line in the central Golan was still far too thin. Accordingly, Northern Command dictated that all reinforcements be directed to the central and southern Golan. Originally, the 679th Reserve Armored Brigade was sent to support the 7th Armored Brigade but was diverted to Nafakh. The 7th Armored Brigade was on its own. After the battle with the Syrian 78th Tank Brigade throughout the morning of Sunday 7 October, the 7th Armored Brigade had destroyed 71 enemy tanks but the Syrians were now biding their time until darkness when they had the advantage of night-fighting equipment. However, the actual infrared equipment was rudimentary and only truly effective at ranges below 500 yards for engaging targets. Furthermore, the driver's IR periscope provided a flat two-dimensional monochromatic image that inhibited depth perception. On the Golan, this was a serious problem with its innumerable boulders and ditches. Many T-54/55s were immobilized on large rocks beneath their belly plates or shed tracks after slipping into unseen depressions. Unlike the Israelis, there was limited recovery or repair facilities for stranded AFVs so even those with minimal damage became booty for the IDF.

During the evening the Sayeret reconnaissance unit was conducting an intelligence-gathering mission in the valley facing the 7th Armored Brigade under the cover of darkness when it encountered a large formation of Syrian armour in its forming-up position. The Sayeret beat a hasty retreat while informing Colonel Ben-Gal of their discovery. On their heels came the largest Syrian assault so far against the 7th Armored Brigade with a force of some 300 tanks. The battle raged until 0100 hours when the Syrians withdrew leaving scores of tanks burning or abandoned. There were now 130 knocked-out Syrian tanks and numerous other AFVs in front of the 7th Armored Brigade's positions in what the Israeli crews called 'the Graveyard'; later it was to be known as the 'Valley of Tears'. But this respite came at a cost. One by one the Shot Cals withdrew to refuel and rearm with ammunition. Medical teams moved forward to evacuate the dead and wounded from the tanks hit on the firing ramps closely followed by the forward repair teams to retrieve the damaged tanks and return them to service as quickly as possible.

On Monday 8 October, the third day of the war, the 77th Tank Battalion made a sweep through the Graveyard to harass the enemy and prevent him from recovering any AFVs or equipment. For the first time, they encountered a Sagger Anti-Tank Guided Missile as well as the usual heavy artillery, with one tank being hit by Sagger and another by an artillery shell that killed the commander, Sergeant Zelig Haberman. Thereafter, the Shot Cals returned to their firing ramps to wait for the next Syrian offensive. During the afternoon, the injured Lieutenant Colonel Yos Eldar arrived at the brigade against doctors' orders. Both he and Shmuel Askarov had escaped form the hospital in Safed to return to their units. To Askarov's horror the 188th Armored Brigade no longer existed but he immediately began collecting crews and tanks to raise the Barak from the ashes. Meanwhile, following the death of Colonel Ben-Shoham and his senior staff, the remnants of the 82nd Tank Battalion joined the 7th Armored Brigade. Similary, Captain Chessner of Company Bet followed suit and together with their 17 tanks set off for the 7th Armored Brigade logistic depot at Wasset Junction. Reinforcements were now pouring on to the Golan including the 146th Reserve Division of Brigadier General Moshe 'Musa' Peled and the 240th Reserve Division of Brigadier General Dan Laner. But, apart from the stragglers from the 82nd Tank Battalion, there were still no reinforcements for the 7th Armored.

On the afternoon of 7 October, the Syrian high command held a fateful meeting at Katana some 25 miles behind the Purple Line. The decision was taken to halt the advance of all units on the southern Golan to allow them to reorganize and await reinforcements before a final offensive was launched on Tuesday. Only in the north was the offensive to continue with the 7th Infantry Division to attack that evening followed by the 3rd Armored Division as soon as they arrived at the front. Thus, the Syrians were reinforcing failure in the north rather than their success in the south. At dusk fell the tanks of the 7th Infantry Division formed up for yet another assault against the 7th Armored Brigade. The GOC of the division, Brigadier Omar Abrash, was well forward with his troops readying his armour for the attack when an Israeli shell killed him. The attack was postponed until the following morning. It gave the 7th Armored Brigade a welcome respite to repair many of their battle casualties and for the tank crews to rest before the next battle; Tuesday was to be the decisive day in the war on the Golan Heights since the Syrians were committing their elite units in a final bid for victory.

ISRAELI DEFENSIVE STRUCTURES ON THE PURPLE LI[N]

Mutzav

anti-tank ditch

firing ramp

THE VALLEY OF TEARS

At dawn on 9 October, the Syrians attacked in great force. Once again, the assault was directed through the valley between Hermonit and Booster. The Shot Cals were already in hull-down positions on their firing ramps but under intense artillery fire. To the north between Hermonit and Bukata were the depleted ranks of the 71st Battalion under the command of Lieutenant Colonel Meshulam Rattes, with just seven serviceable tanks and to the south was the 77th near Booster with the remnants of the 74th and 82nd covering Kuneitra: a total of 34 tanks in all. As battle was joined and the enemy intentions became apparent, Colonel Ben-Gal ordered Khahalani to deploy his seven remaining tanks close to brigade headquarters at Yakir-Kirton as a second line of defence. The Seventh was in a vice. To their front, the valley floor was now inundated with some 100 T-62s of the 81st Tank Brigade from the 3rd Armoured Division. The fighting was desperate on the central sector where the Shot Cals were being inexorably whittled away by artillery damage and hyper-velocity fin-stabilized tungsten bolts that ripped through armour plate with deadly effect. Such was the intensity of fire that Ben-Gal allowed the tanks to withdraw from the ramps to escape the worst of the shelling. The intention was that when the barrage lifted, the tanks would resume their positions on the ramps but the Syrians were advancing relentlessly within yards of the bombardment. Their tanks had every chance of getting there first. Yos Eldar and his vunerable APCs were obliged to fall back further because of the massive artillery barrage.

ISRAELI GUNNER'S VIEW

SYRIAN GUNNER'S VIEW

Israeli tank gunners were uniformly superior to their Syrian counterparts thanks in part to the superior optical sights of the Centurion as shown here as a T-55 is hit at close range viewed through the gunner's Sight Periscopic No.30.

The TSh 2-22 gunner's sight has a magnification of X3.5 or X7 but in the final battles of the Syrian offensive the tanks were so close that range assessment was unnecessary and opposing AFVs often filled the gunner's field of view, but only if they left the safety of the firing ramps.

Realizing the danger, Ben-Gall ordered Kahalani to advance towards the ramps. The fighting was now at close quarters and any tank hit at such ranges was sure to be destroyed, usually exploding in ball of flame. Survival was dependent on quick reactions and the ability of the crews to acquire targets, load the correct type of ammunition and fire with accuracy in the shortest possible time. Throughout the four days of battle, Israeli crews proved far more proficient in tank gunnery than their Syrian counterparts, often firing ten rounds a minute in the Shot Cal as against four in the T-54/55 or T-62. Kahalani and his crew alone succeeded in destroying five T-62s in five minutes. Yet still the Syrians advanced with great fortitude. From his position, Kahalani was able to see down into the valley where he could see hundreds of tanks massing. These tanks belonged to the elite Republican Guard commanded by Rifaat Assad, brother of the Syrian President Hafez Assad. Both sides realized that this was the last throw of the dice and victory or defeat was now at hand.

For the 7th Armored Brigade, it was critical to regain these dominating firing ramps if the Syrians were to be stopped. The tank crews were emotionally drained and exhausted after almost four days of fighting, without proper sleep or food and under constant bombardment from artillery and air attack. The Shot Cals had survived numerous duels with T-54/55s but now in the final hours of the war, it seemed as if they would be overwhelmed by the hordes of T-62s. For the last four days, Colonel Ben-Gal had led his brigade with the surest touch, encouraging and cajoling his men calmly yet firmly, while always retaining a reserve of tanks, however small. These were fed into battle at critical moments and then another reserve was immediately formed from other assets in the brigade. In reality, companies or battalions no longer meant anything, as platoons moved here and there as the situation demanded, plugging into a different radio net as directed for however long before redeploying to another sector or unit. It was a measure of the professionalism and flexibility of the crews and their commanders. Coupled with the Herculean efforts of the forward repair teams, battle-damaged Shot Cals were quickly returned to service since the brigade was denied any reinforcements at all. Similarly, the wounded or dead were never left on the battlefield but were evacuated to the hard-pressed medical staff as soon as possible. All the while, logistic personnel drove their unprotected trucks through shot and shell to ensure a constant supply of fuel and ammunition. Ammunition was the key. The tanks had fired so many rounds that their gun barrels were shot out and were no longer accurate at long range, but the engagement distances were now measured in scores of yards at most.

Refused permission to withdraw, some reinforcements did arrive thanks to Major Shmuel Askarov who had discharged himself from hospital, together with Yos Eldar, on Monday morning. Once back on the Golan, he gathered tanks and men from a variety of shattered units. He was joined by Lieutenant Colonel Yossi Ben-Hanan, who had been the commander of the 53rd Tank Battalion until a month ago. The 53rd Tank Battalion of the Barak Brigade was born again. With the codename 'Morning Exercise', the patchwork force moved off to help the 7th Armored Brigade in its desperate plight. In the meantime, the remaining tanks resisted attempts to position themselves on the ramps. One sergeant did offer to move forward but he was already out of ammunition. Realizing that direct orders were having no effect, Kahalani resorted to shaming his men into action:

> Shoter stations. This is the battalion commander. Look at the courage of the enemy mounting the position in front of us. I don't know what's happening to us. They are only the enemy we have always known. We are stronger than them. Start moving forward and form a line with me. I am waving my flag. Move!

Slowly the Shot Cals began to stir, gathering pace until a solid line was formed with just the heads of the tank commanders visible in the turrets. A T-62 loomed over the ramp but was instantly hit. The line of Shot Cals weaved their way around the burning wrecks of friend and foe alike until they reached the firing ramps. The Shot Cals opened fire with precisely aimed, rapid fire. Geva's tanks soon arrived on the firing ramps and added their weight of fire and were then joined by Lieutenant Colonel Ben-Hanan's forces. Topping the next rise, Ben-Hanan saw a T-55 just 50 yards away. Shouting to his driver to stop, he ordered his gunner to fire. The Barak Brigade was back in the war. Battle was joined at close quarters with Israeli and Syrian tanks hopelessly intermingled but gradually the Syrians were forced back and the attack was broken, but at a cost. Both Ben-Hanan and Askarov were injured; Askarov critically with a gunshot wound to the head. Shortly afterwards, an observer in Mutzav 107 reported that the Syrian column of vehicles across the Purple Line was turning round and AFVs were falling back from the 'Valley of Tears'. The battle was over. The 7th Armored Brigade and the 188th Barak Armored Brigade had prevailed against overwhelming odds. As the battle subsided, the commander of the 36th Armored Division, Brigadier General Raful Eitan, came on the 7th Armored Brigade radio net and announced: 'You have saved the people of Israel.'

A mortally wounded tank commander is lifted from the turret of a Shot Cal after being struck in the throat by fragments from a Sagger missile. During the Israeli counter-offensive, the Sagger ATGM was used in large numbers and some tanks were festooned with the missiles' guidance wires. (IGPO)

AFTERMATH

OPPOSITE
The last occasion that the Centurion fought the T-55 was during the protracted Angolan civil war in 1987–88 in southwest Africa. Manned mainly by Cubans, the T-55s were once again comprehensively outclassed by the modernized Centurions that are called Olifant in the South African Defence Force. Like Israeli Centurions, the Olifant Mk IA features a Continental V-12 750hp diesel engine and a semi-automatic transmission with a locally produced version of the L7 105mm gun as well as a new fire control system and passive night sights. This Olifant Mk IA or Elephant in Afrikaans is shown in the typical harsh bush terrain of Namibia and Angola during the final stages of the war against the FAPLA and their Cuban allies in June 1988. The SADF currently employ the Olifant Mk IB that remains a formidable Main Battle Tank in the early 21st Century: a remarkable testimony to a design that originated in 1943. (William Surmon)

By midday on Wednesday 10 October 1973, the Israeli counterattack in the central sector forced the last remaining Syrian units back across the Purple Line. The defence of the Golan Plateau in the opening days of the Yom Kippur War was undoubtedly the IDF's most difficult campaign since the War of Independence in 1948–49. For the first time, the ground forces had fought without air superiority or close air support from the Israeli Air Force; enduring repeated sorties by Syrian ground attack aircraft. The scale of casualties in men and matériel was unprecedented, with the Israeli Armored Corps suffering most. Almost 75 per cent of the tank crewmen in the 7th Armored Brigade were either killed or wounded in the first four days of the war: many of them tank commanders. At its lowest ebb, it possessed just nine tanks but, within 24 hours of the final battle overlooking the Valley of Tears, the brigade strength rose to 100 tanks with many replacement crews drawn from the reservists. The 188th Barak Armored Brigade suffered even more casualties in men and machines yet it too grew like a phoenix out of the ashes and burnt-out tank hulks dotted along the Purple Line to fight again. After lengthy deliberations throughout Wednesday afternoon, the Israeli government decided that the IDF must cross the Purple Line and capture a swathe of Syrian territory before the imposition of any ceasefire. The attack was to be launched on Thursday 11 October and the two units to lead the assault were to be the 7th and 188th Armored Brigades. It is axiomatic that any military unit that suffers more than 33 per cent casualties in any given battle is fit for future operations only after a period of rest and recuperation, yet the 36th Armored Division led the Israeli counteroffensive into Syria after just 18 hours of reorganization. Within three days, Israeli forces and long-range artillery were threatening the outskirts of Damascus. It was a remarkable testament to the fortitude, flexibility and motivation of the IDF and the men of the Israeli Armored Corps.

It was these attributes that allowed a force of just 177 Shot Cals to resist the concerted offensive of 1,400 Syrian tanks over a period of 81 hours without reinforcement and with hardly any sleep or respite under the incessant artillery bombardment. There is no doubt that the IDF high command was highly remiss in allowing such a disparity of forces to exist on the Golan Plateau yet this was also due to the masterly deception plan mounted by the Egyptians and Syrians in order to gain strategic surprise for their joint offensive against Israel. In the final analysis, it was the courage and resolve of the individual tank crews that determined the outcome of the defensive battle rather than any contingency planning by the IDF. Similarly the Syrian tank crews, mostly in their T-54/55s but also T-62s, fought with a grim tenacity never witnessed before by the Israelis. However, they too were let down by their high command. The Syrians were well aware of the Israeli dispositions on the Golan Plateau and intended to swamp the defences by overwhelming numbers of tanks on a broad front along the entire length of the Purple Line. Nevertheless, the lack of tactical flexibility at the brigade and regimental level did not allow for any deviation from the overall plan, whether it was to bypass particularly determined Israeli defences or capitalise on the superior night-fighting capability of their Soviet tank designs.

The greatest mistake remained the failure to reinforce the success of the attack in the southern Golan rather than continuing to batter the 7th Armored Brigade in the north. The fault lay with requiring the field commanders to leave the frontlines for consultation with the high command at Katana some 25 miles away. The time lag between a decision being taken and then implemented on at the front did not match the unfolding events on the ground.

Conversely, the Israeli command and control system was flexible and rapid, once the initial shock of the massive offensive was overcome. At the brigade level, Colonel Yanosh Ben-Gal kept close behind his fighting units and was in constant communications with them. At all times, he attempted to maintain a reserve force, however small, to be committed at critical points and junctures as the situation demanded. Furthermore, he quickly recognized the scale of the Syrian offensive and the indecisive response of Northern Command on the first day. Accordingly, he did not allow any of his units to be diverted elsewhere, despite orders from above to do so to ensure as much cohesion as possible. There were simply not enough tanks to allow any further dispersal and throughout the battle he sought the recall of the 82nd Tank Battalion to his command: a move that was to prove critical on the morning of 9 October in the final battle of the Kuneitra Gap. On the southern sector, Colonel Yitzhak Ben-Shoham was not informed by the high command of the likelihood of a full-scale Syrian offensive on Yom Kippur. Instead, he remained at the command headquarters at Nafekh trying to conduct a different type of battle and thus separated from his frontline units. When he attempted to join them in the early evening, the Syrians had already broken through and so he was unable to link up with his brigade. Whether he could have done anything differently given the disparity of forces is debatable and the gallant officer paid the ultimate sacrifice in the defence of his country.

The GOC of Northern Command, Major General Yitzhak Hofi, came in for criticism of his handling of the campaign in the opening days of the war. He had been concerned about the disparity of forces on the Golan for sometime and voiced his dismay to the General Staff. He was particularly worried by the threat posed by the Syrian mobile anti-aircraft batteries of SA-6 missiles. He feared that the air force would be unable to provide the essential close air support to the ground troops in the event of attack. But like the Israeli General Staff he did not believe that there was any real prospect of all-out war. Nevertheless, he authorized the extension and refurbishment of the anti-tank defences along the Purple Line as well as the creation of more tracks across the Golan to allow the better provision of supplies by wheeled vehicles to the frontlines. Crucially, he also authorized the construction of more firing ramps on the Hermonit and Booster hill features overlooking the Kuneitra Gap. These simple earth mounds, together with those already built beside the infantry strong-points, were to prove of decisive importance during the defensive battle. Hofi's fears prompted General Moshe Dayan to request the deployment of the 7th Armored Brigade to the Golan Heights on the eve of Rosh Hoshana.

The role of Israeli artillery, whose sustained barrage helped to break the will of the attackers, was crucial to her defence but it was the crews of the Shot Cals and the

T-54/55s that bore the brunt of the war on the Golan. Israeli casualties on the Golan were 772 dead and 2,453 wounded, mostly from the armoured corps. The Syrians lost 3,500 dead and 5,600 wounded together with 348 prisoners of war.

The battlefield was also littered with hundreds of Syrian AFVs. Of the 1,400 tanks committed to battle, 1,181 were disabled during the war as well as 50 Iraqi and 20 Jordanian tanks. Of these 867 were left on the Golan Plateau, including 627 T-54/55s and 240 T-62s. Many of these were abandoned by their crews and were recovered intact by the Israelis and pressed into IDF service after modification as the 'Tiran'. Of those that were knocked out in battle, 80 per cent were destroyed by 105mm tank fire, 10 per cent were disabled by the anti-tank obstacles, mines, artillery or airpower with a further 10 per cent by guided weapons and HEAT projectiles. The T-54/55, as well as the T-62, tanks featured remarkably thick armour for such a compact design and their excellent ballistic shape made them difficult to penetrate at the ranges favoured for engagement by Israeli tank crews. The specialist AFVs such as the bridge-layers and mine-clearing tanks were the priority targets and engaged at between 2,500 and 3,000 yards. However, 70 per cent of all engagements were below 2,000 yards. Overall of those tanks hit by 105mm tank fire, 50 per cent were penetrated of which most caught fire. The combination of fuel and ammunition stowed in the front hull beside the driver proved particularly vulnerable to fire even without full penetration when hit by APDS rounds.

Conversely, IDF statistics reveal that 680 Centurions were deployed on the Golan of which two-thirds were Shot Cal and the remainder Shot Meteor. Of the 200 Shot

A Shot Cal lies rent asunder by an internal explosion during the fighting of 7 October near Nafakh. Statistically, every Israeli tank employed on the Golan was hit 1.5 times and approximately 100 were completely destroyed, such as this one. (IGPO)

After the Shot Cal was withdrawn from service as a gun tank, it was converted into several special purpose variants as heavy APCs that were more resistant to attacks from mines and IEDs than standard APCs such as the Mii3 series. The Shot Cal also became a successful vehicle for combat engineers under the designation Puma from *Poretz Mokshim Handasati*, literally, 'breakthrough mine engineer vehicle'. With a crew of up to eight combat engineers, the Puma can be configured with various breaching and assault systems such as dozer blade, mineroller or the Carpet rocket-propelled fuel-air explosive minefield demolition charge. This version shown on exercise on the Golan Plateau in 2001 has an RKM mineroller device. (IGPO)

Cals engaged in the first few days, each was hit on average one and a half times by ordnance of various types and of those struck by 100mm and 115mm projectiles, 29 per cent were penetrated of which 25 per cent caught fire. During the course of the war on the Golan, 250 Shot and Sherman tanks were knocked out but of these 150 were returned to service after rebuilding and refurbishment.

During the defensive battle in the northern sector, the 7th Armored Brigade destroyed some 500 AFVs of which 260 were T-54/55 and T-62 tanks. Ammunition expenditure was huge. Each Shot Cal carried 72 rounds of main armament ammunition but after each battle day, 45 per cent of tanks had less than 10 rounds left and the remainder less than 20. But it was superior gunnery techniques that proved ultimately decisive: the true legacy of General Israel 'Talik' Tal. The close coordination between the average Shot tank crew, few of whom were over 20 years of age, allowed a sustained rate of accurate fire, particularly when perched on the dominating firing ramps. Israeli crews consistently enjoyed a range advantage of 500 to 1,000 yards thanks to superior training and sighting equipment. Coupled with better leadership and high motivation given the perceived threat to Israel's existence, the Israeli Armored Corps performed in an outstanding manner and by the end of the war their tanks were threatening both the Arab capitals of Cairo and Damascus. Those who stopped the Syrian onslaught were not volunteers from elite units but ordinary tank crews who represented a cross-section of society. The nation proved strong enough to survive the failures of its leadership. Similarly, the Shot Cal proved strong enough to resist the T-54/55 in combat and triumph in arguably the greatest defensive battle in the annals of armoured warfare.

BIBLIOGRAPHY

Dunstan, Simon, *Centurion* (London, Ian Allan Ltd, 1980)

Dunstan, Simon, *Centurion Universal Tank 1943–2003* (Oxford, Osprey, 2003)

Eshel, David and Dunstan, Simon, *Centurion Main Battle Tank* (Israel, Eshel Dramit Ltd, 1979)

Eshel, David, *Chariots of the Desert: The Story of the Israeli Armoured Corps* (London, Brassey's, 1989)

Fletcher, David, *Mechanised Force: British Tanks between the Wars* (London, HMSO, 1991)

Kahalani, Avigdor, *The Heights of Courage: A Tank Leader's War on the Golan* (London, Praeger, 1992)

Kahalani, Avigdor, *A Warrior's Way* (Israel, Steimatzky,1999)

Norman, Michael, *Soviet Mediums T-44, T-54, T-55 and T-62* (Profile Publications Ltd, 1978)

Rabinovich, Abraham, *The Yom Kippur War: The Epic Encounter that Transformed the Middle East* (New York, Schocken Books, 2004)

Rabinovich, Abraham, *Stemming the Syrian Onslaught – Abraham Rabinovich* (The Quarterly Journal of Military History, Spring 2001)

Rabinovich, Abraham, *Shattered Heights* (Jerusalem Post), Israel, 25 September 1998 and 2 October 1998

Teveth, Shabtai, *The Tanks of Tammuz* (London, Weidenfeld and Nicholson, 1969)

Zaloga, Steven J., *Armour of the Middle East Wars 1948–78* (London, Osprey, 1981)

Zaloga, Steven J., *Modern Soviet Armour Combat Vehicles of the USSR and Warsaw Pact Today* (London, Arms and Armour Press, 1979)

Zaloga, Steven J., *Modern Soviet Combat Tanks* (London, Osprey, 1984)

INDEX